# Literary Formations

# Interpretations

This series provides clearly written and up-to-date introductions to recent theories and critical practices in the humanities and social sciences.

General Editor
Ken Ruthven (University of Melbourne)

Advisory Board
Tony Bennett (Griffith University)
Penny Boumelha (University of Adelaide)
John Frow (University of Queensland)
Sneja Gunew (University of Victoria, British Columbia)
Kevin Hart (Monash University)
Robert Hodge (University of Western Sydney)
Terry Threadgold (Monash University)

In preparation:
The body in the text, by Anne Cranny-Francis
Reconstructing theory, edited by David Roberts
After a fashion, by Joanne Finkelstein
Hypertext, by Ilana Snyder
German feminist theory, by Silke Beinssen-Hesse
and Catherine Rigby

# Literary Formations

## Post-colonialism, Nationalism, Globalism

Anne Brewster

MELBOURNE UNIVERSITY PRESS
1995

Melbourne University Press
PO Box 278, Carlton South, Victoria 3053, Australia

First published 1995

Designed by Mark Davis/text-art
Typeset by Melbourne University Press in 10.5/13 pt Garamond
Printed in Malaysia by SRM Production Services Sdn Bhd

ISSN 1039-6128

National Library of Australia Cataloguing-in-Publication entry

Brewster, Anne.
  Literary formations: post-colonialism, nationalism,
  globalism
  Bibliography.
  Includes index.
  ISBN 0 522 84534 7.
  1. Australian prose literature—Aboriginal authors—History
  and criticism. 2. Australian prose literature—Women authors—
  History and criticism. 3. Autobiography—Women authors.
  4. Aborigines Australian—Women—Biography—History and
  criticism. 5. English prose literature—20th century—History and
  criticism. 6. English prose literature—Minority authors—
  History and criticism. 7. Decolonization in literature.
  8. Nationalism in literature. 9. Postmodernism (Literature).
  10. Feminism and literature. I. Title. (Series: Interpretations).
  828.08

# Contents

# Contents

# Acknowledgements

I would like to thank Curtin University for a research grant which enabled me to start the research for this book; I am especially grateful to Don Grant, Head of the School of Communication and Cultural Studies, for his support, and to Rae Kelly, Helen Mumme, Noreen Richards and Sally Carter for their constant helpfulness and cheerfulness. I would also like to thank Peter Lavskis for his generosity and patience; Sneja Gunew who encouraged me to begin this project; and Ken Ruthven and Susan Keogh for their editorial rigour and expertise.

I am grateful to the following colleagues for reading various parts of the book in manuscript and making helpful comments: Hugh Webb, Rod Giblett, Rosemary van den Berg, Mudrooroo, Vijay Mishra, Kathy Trees, Joan Newman and Pat Dudgeon; and to my honours students who graciously gave me space during my mid-year teaching break in 1993 to work on the manuscript.

I would also like to thank Vicki Brimmell, Cynthia Yasbincek, Brigid Lowry, Alison Georgeson and in particular, Catherine Breen who helped me at various stages in my attenuated research; Ron Blaber for the generous loan of a computer; Ross Bennett for his encouragement; David Buchbinder for his advice on points of style; Les Kinnane for looking after my house during my frequent and extended absences; and Linda Browning for her time and her fine intelligence, perfectionism and good humour, which were invaluable in assisting me to prepare the manuscript for publication.

Parts of chapters 2, 3 and 5 appeared in different form in *Australia in the World*, D. Grant and G. Seal (eds), Perth: Black Swan Press, 1994; *Kunapipi* XVI, 1, 1994; and *SPAN* 34–5, October 1992/May 1993 respectively; my thanks to the editors.

*For my parents*

*Helen Robinson Brewster*
*and*
*John Arthur Stewart Brewster*

# 1

# Themes

*I chose to survive and am living to tell my tale*
Rosemary van den Berg

This book focuses on minority groups and the ways they are managed by the dominant culture. Contemporary Australia is a nation formed by colonisation and immigration; it is a stage for the disinheritance, displacement and dispossession of both indigenous and immigrant peoples. Diaspora and migration are normative and customary in this age of large-scale population movements in the wake of decolonisation and the global influence of transnational corporations. Notions of homelands and origins are as troubling and problematic for some people as those of post-coloniality and nationalism. Post-coloniality takes different forms in different countries. In non-'settler' countries, independence has provided the opportunity for self-determination; in 'settler' (or 'invader') countries such as Australia, indigenous peoples remain culturally colonised and subordinate. 'Post-colonial' is a term with limited viability for these constituencies, that is, for these groups of people marked out as such by power relations with the dominant culture.

However, now that the formerly invisible history of indigenous people has come to intervene in the public domain, there has been a transformation in the way non-Aboriginal Australians think about both the past and the construction of the nation. As the history and structures of colonisation continue to be exposed by the narratives of Aboriginal people, strategies of decolonisation and self-determination are set in motion. Consequently, non-Aboriginal people are experiencing a crisis of identity. Just as Aboriginal narratives radically problematise concepts of 'discovery', 'settlement' and 'sovereignty', narratives of diaspora and immigration likewise interrogate official and stereotypic constructions of origin, ethnicity and multiculturalism.

Those whom the dominant culture deems 'other' render national certainties fragile and indeterminate. Just as vigorously, however, the discourse of nationalism re-territorialises and absorbs these constituencies. I examine the staging of nationalism in the arena of Australian literary studies, and in particular how two bodies of writing—autobiographical narratives by Aboriginal women such as Ruby Langford Ginibi, Alice Nannup and Evelyn Crawford, and works by the Polish-Australian, Ania Walwicz—resist discourses of nationalism and post-colonialism. Two further case studies, Philip Jeyaretnam in Singapore and Bharati Mukherjee in the USA, illustrate how ethnic minority writers elsewhere negotiate similar discourses. I look also at formations of nationalism in the work of the Singaporean poet, Arthur Yap. As a Chinese he is from the dominant ethnic group, and his critique of nationalism focuses not so much on issues of ethnicity as on everyday life and people's lived experience. In a postmodern age of global population flows, immigrant and indigenous people do not exist in isolated communities. Just as immigrant people have global links with other cultures and places, Aboriginal people with common histories of colonisation have pan-Aboriginal and pan-indigenous affiliations. In this Introduction, I want to explore those key concepts of 'post-colonialism', 'nationalism' and 'globalism' which inform the discussion that follows.

## Aboriginality and the formation of identity

The late twentieth century is often described as having a 'memorial' or 'museal' sensibility on account of its obsession with the past. Andreas Huyssen characterises postmodern temporality as hovering between 'the need for remembering and the fast track for forgetting'. 'Our culture's undisputed tendency towards amnesia', he suggests, is 'motivated by immediate profit and political expediency' (Huyssen, 1994:12). (It should be noted at this point that he doesn't specify the identity of 'our'.) He goes on to remark that remembrance shapes people's links with the past, and that the ways they remember define these links in the present (ibid.:9). As a result of this dialogue between the past and the present, our present has an impact on what and how we remember.

The structure and contents of memory are contingent upon the social formations that produce them. The place and form of memory in any culture are a result of many complex political, historical and psychological factors (ibid.:9–11). The encounter with colonial violence shapes Aboriginal memory in specific and persistent ways. Given that past—and the conditions of poverty, violence, incarceration and racism in which many Aboriginal people continue to live—in some ways Aboriginal remembrance functions differently from the postmodern memory that Huyssen analyses. Debbie Rose describes Aboriginal remembrance as the '*living* experience of the past, regenerated through stories' which sustain relationships with it (Rose, 1992:15); 'as long as the conditions of the past are the conditions of the present,' she says, 'then the past is not past (ibid.:17). She suggests that, to live in 'the richness of the present', Aboriginal people need to engage actively with their past, even though this means 'assent[ing] to the necessity of loss' (ibid.:15). Jackie Huggins has also remarked upon Aboriginal people's different awareness of the past: 'Aboriginal writers', she says, 'have a stronger sense of history than their white counterparts' (1993:62). Arthur Corunna, Sally Morgan's great-uncle, puts it another way: 'the black man's got a long memory', he says (Morgan, 1987:210). Peter Burke illuminates further the different relationships minority and dominant cultures have with the past:

> It is often said that history is written by the victors. It might also be said that history is forgotten by the victors. They can afford to forget, while the losers are unable to accept what happened and are condemned to brood over it, relive it, and reflect how different it might have been. (Burke, 1989:106)

For Aboriginal people memory has a political and cultural significance different from that of both 'settlers' and immigrants.

Deprived of their land, and forced to endure the status of people systematically categorised as 'naturally inferior', Aboriginal people have had limited access to the cultural capital of their heritage (Bottomley, 1992:6). Paul Gilroy (1991:13) points out that the memory of slavery among the peoples of the 'black Atlantic' is 'actively preserved as a living intellectual resource in their expressive political culture'. This is equally true of Aboriginal people in Australia. Like the people of the black Atlantic, they sustain the memory of a rarely acknowledged history of slavery and labour exploitation that, as Aboriginal women attest in their autobiographical narratives, was the foundation of the Australian pastoral industry. Aboriginal memory preserves the unwritten black history of colonisation, which has been emerging into the public arena in the form of life stories of Aboriginal women. Aboriginal memory is transforming public perceptions of the past in post-invasion Australia. Yet as Paul Gilroy (1993) has suggested, the people of the black Atlantic are not simply the passive victims or onlookers of modernity, but rather the producers and makers of modern Euro-American society through their slave labour. The same may be said of the Aboriginal heritage in modern Australia.

According to Stuart Hall, identity is formed at the point where 'the "unspeakable" stories of subjectivity meet the narratives of history', and, we might add, 'the nation' (Hall, 1987:44). Huyssen likewise regards the horror, humiliation and degradation experienced by victims of the Holocaust as fundamentally 'unspeakable' and 'unrepresentable' (Huyssen, 1994:16). The genocidal invasion of Australia produced a history of terror similar to that of the Holocaust. Until recently, this Aboriginal history was not speakable: there was no site upon which it could enter the public domain, and no means by which it could be heard within the dominant culture. In discussing Queensland politics, Jackie Huggins (quoting Raymond Evans) makes the point that before the first political organisation involving Aboriginal people was formed in 1960—QCAATSI, the Queensland Council for the Advancement of Aboriginal and Torres Strait Islanders —not a single statement from an Aboriginal was ever reproduced in parliament, in a printed government report, or in the media (Huggins, 1991b:145). Yet Aboriginal subjectivity is now emerging in ways that are rewriting the history of this country. Stories that have been 'unspeakable' since 1788 are appearing in print. Aboriginal women's autobiographical histories are corporeal histories of the gendered and racialised body that has been placed under surveillance, disciplined, silenced and condemned to poverty. Their histories are of rape and abuse, childbearing and motherhood, extended family networks, the absence of male partners, arduous physical labour and political activism. As such they embody the history of the making of modern Australia, and the survival of Aboriginal culture into the twenty-first century. John Gillis (1992:100) talks about the domestication and feminisation of memory in mainstream culture; interestingly, a similar trend can be discerned in contemporary Aboriginal culture. In a review of recent literature on public memory and history, Gillis also argues that we are entering an era of post-national memory. If this is so, it is the emerging memories of Aboriginal and immigrant minorities that are problematising the foundations of the national past.

The 'unspeakable stories' of Aboriginal memory and their radical subjectivity have emerged at a specific time in global history. Hall observes that 'black is an identity which had to be learned and could only be learned in a certain moment' (1987:45). In Jamaica that moment was the 1970s, when the Afro-Caribbean identity became historically available to black Jamaicans at home and abroad through 'the impact on popular life of the post-colonial revolution, the civil rights struggles, the culture of Rastafarianism and the music of reggae' (Hall, 1990:231). In Australia, on the other hand, Aboriginal people first developed a visible political identity in the 1960s. Australians had been affected from the 1940s onwards by the decolonising and independence movements in South and South-east Asia and Africa. The effect on the new left of these global changes and the American civil rights movement was to introduce a new Aboriginal subjectivity into white Australian culture. The success, for example, of the first book of Aboriginal poetry—*We Are Going* (1964) by Kath Walker (Oodgeroo Noonuccal), which established her as the best-selling Australian poet after C. J. Dennis— was evidence of the growing visibility of Aboriginal people. Moreover, the new access to print of leading Aboriginal activists such as Walker (as she was known in the 1960s and 1970s) facilitated the development of a pan-Aboriginality (Brewster, 1994).

The activism of the 1960s led to the establishment in the 1970s of Aboriginal legal, health, media and education services, as well as some success with land-rights claims. Jackie Huggins states that 'of all the protest movements in Australia, that for Aboriginal rights has been the most persistent and widespread' (Huggins, 1991b:162). Aboriginal resistance and the struggle for Aboriginal voices to be heard have taken many different forms since the European invasion. As Joan Scott observes, 'subjects are produced through multiple identifications, some of which become politically salient for a time in certain contexts' (Scott, 1992:19). Contemporary Aboriginality is one such identification, and it has proven effective in harnessing the cultural capital of Aboriginal memory in order to produce a nation-wide sense of solidarity and common interest among Aboriginal people. (For further discussion of the deployment of the concept of Aboriginality, see John Fielder, 1991; Tim Rowse, 1985; Marcia Langton, 1993 and 1994.) Aboriginality has thus been an effective counter-discourse to the epistemic violence of colonisation (that is, the manner in which the colonial subject constructs knowledge of the other). Yet colonialism is only one of a number of formations which determine identity; others include class and gender. Poverty is an experience that Aboriginal women's autobiographies unfailingly illustrate. It permeates racial divisions. Many Aboriginal women have commented on experiences shared with poor whites, and the class solidarity produced by poverty. Ruby Langford Ginibi, for example, describing poverty in *Don't Take Your Love to Town*, writes that 'plenty of people lived like that, poor whites as well as blacks' (Langford, 1988:84). Similarly, Rita Huggins, in her collaborative autobiographical narrative, *Auntie Rita*, portrays the shared poverty of Aboriginals and whites in the 1950s in the Brisbane suburb of Inala (Huggins and Huggins, 1994:75), and Ella Simon in her autobiographical narrative *Through My Eyes* describes how, in her grandfather's time, 'There wasn't much difference between us and poor white people' (1978:26). And like class, gender is often left out of discussions of Aboriginal literature, although it is a determining force in Aboriginal women's narratives. Such elisions can produce a discourse blind to the ideology of its own masculinist and imperialist formation, which, by treating gender an unmarked category, makes it invisible.

# Aboriginal texts, feminism and the academy

In Chapter 3 I discuss an issue that has attracted the attention of mainstream feminists, namely the gendering of the genre of Aboriginal women's autobiographical narratives. How non-Aboriginal women might position themselves in relation to Aboriginal women and their texts is a complex issue. It has become increasingly evident that First World feminism, by focusing exclusively on the issue of gender, has elided issues of class and race, and assumed the universality of female subjectivity. First World feminists are beginning to confront the issue of racism, however, and to become sensitive to the unmarked and unnamed category of 'whiteness' (Frankenberg, 1993). In order to 'unlearn their privilege' and to avoid colonising or appropriating Aboriginal women's knowledge, non-Aboriginal women such as myself can inform and educate themselves about those histories and issues that are of most concern to Aboriginal people. Aboriginal women have stressed the need for consultation before writing or speaking about Aboriginal people. While it is important that non-Aboriginal women neither speak on behalf of nor ventriloquise Aboriginal women, it is also important that we remain open to the possibility of alliances, however provisional and contingent.

As I discuss in Chapter 3, Aboriginal women see their stories as having an educative role for both Aboriginal and non-Aboriginal people, especially in schools and universities. Kath Walker (Oodgeroo Noonuccal) spoke in 1977 about intervening in racism by educating the younger people of the population: 'I'm sick and tired of talking to mentally constipated adults', she told Jim Davidson. 'It's through children that change will come, so we have them [to visit Minjerriba] from the kindergarten stage right through to university students' (Walker, 1977:437). In the classrooms of the educational institution, non-Aboriginal women do indeed have a role to play in addressing racism and circulating Aboriginal women's texts. Sometimes this can be a considerable challenge for women whose own position and representation within the academies are marginal, and whose mobility and power to enact change are correspondingly constrained. The location of women within the academy is thus a cognate issue sometimes rendered invisible in discussions of their teaching practice.

Needless to say, the classroom pedagogy (that is, the practice of teaching) of white middle-class feminists such as myself must be reflexive and politically informed. The so-called 'second-wave' feminism created largely by white women in the late 1960s prompted critiques of its racism by minority feminists, women of colour and indigenous women. The distinctively multi-racial feminisms that emerged in the mid 1970s as a result of those critiques could be described as 'third-wave' feminisms (Frankenberg, 1993:266 n3). Feminism in Australia needs to be responsive to the aims and needs of Aboriginal women. It is a politically sensitive arena in which are staged debates such as that sparked off by an article on rape in Aboriginal communities, written by the radical feminist Diane Bell in collaboration with Topsy Napurrula Nelson (see Bell and Nelson, 1989; Bell, 1991a; Bell, 1991b; Huggins et al., 1991; Larbalestier, 1990; Yeatman, 1993). A more recent case is the Tidda's Manifesto (Felton and Flanagan, 1993), one of the first comprehensive published statements by Aboriginal women proposing conditions for an alliance with white feminists.

There is a tension in this field between separatist and alliance logics. White middle-class feminists, as well as being reflexive about their own speaking position and the way they make spaces for Aboriginal women's knowledges, must examine not only what Edward Said calls 'possessive exclusivism . . . [that is] the sense of being an excluding insider by virtue of experience' (Said, 1985:25) but also what the Chicago Cultural Studies Group calls the 'romance of authenticity' (1992:543). 'Possessive exclusivism' and 'the romance of authenticity' both play on the idea of guilt whose silencing effect (discussed in Chapter 3) is passive and disabling. Gayatri Spivak suggests that as an alternative to guilt you can

> develop a certain degree of rage against the history that has written such an abject script for you that you are silenced . . . Then you begin to investigate what it is that silences you, rather than take this very deterministic position—since my skin colour is this, since my sex is this, I cannot speak. I call these things, as you know, somewhat derisively, chromatism: basing everything

on skin colour—'I am white, I can't speak' . . . To say 'I won't criticise' is salving your conscience, and allowing you not to do any homework. (Spivak, 1990a:62–3)

If non-Aboriginal academics are to play a role in circulating Aboriginal texts, it is important that they do adequate 'homework' and undertake research in a consultative manner (see Little, 1993). Teaching and writing practices that are not consultative, dialogic and interactive may run the risk of becoming altogether alienated from the Aboriginal constituency which is the object of its knowledge production, thereby exploiting and appropriating Aboriginal people's knowledge. As Patricia Mamajun Torres points out:

> over the last few hundred years Indigenous Australians have provided copious amounts of information for PhDs, research theses, governmental reviews etc., but few have ever benefited personally in terms of financial or academic gains. This situation is in part due to the fact that many people who have provided specialised information to academics and others have not been seen as co-authors, writers or owners of the information or the copyright holders. (Torres, 1994:25)

The Chicago Cultural Studies Group (CCSG) elaborates on how feminists are accountable to those they speak for and about:

> The multiple publics of feminism continue to pressure academic feminists not to become too invested in professional rhetorics of expertise, too limited by the norms of academic rational discourse, too constrained by values about what constitutes arguments and evidence, too focused on the pseudo-meritocracy of ideas that academia promises. (CCSG, 1992:547)

The CCSG argues for 'affiliated knowledges' which maintain their link with constituencies outside the academy. In this way, the position of academics relative to such constituencies is made visible: Aboriginal women's knowledge, for example, does not then become subsumed into a humanistic discourse orchestrated by a universal academic authority. The academic's own position is not seen as unproblematic, but rather as a site of conflict. The process of negotiating a speaking position is dialogic. A 'space-clearing' procedure which opens up a site of difference within the academy, it therefore enables white middle-class academics to be reflexive about their pedagogy and the way they frame Aboriginal texts. Aboriginal people, for example, have questioned the colonising and exclusionary effects of post-structuralist theory and its negating of identity politics. The CCSG cautions against 'an overconfidence in the ability of theory to master and translate different points of view, resulting in criticism that confirms the elasticity of dominant discourse rather than providing a point of access for marginal groups' (CCSG, 1992:542–3).

This is not to suggest that post-structuralist and postmodernist theory are wholly irrelevant to discussions of Aboriginal texts (see Narogin, 1990). Minority groups, including indigenous peoples, have identified points of congruence between discussions of postmodernist subjectivity and their own issues of identity, as I explain below and in Chapter 4. We might describe the intervention of Aboriginal discourse into critical theory as the 'indigenisation' of theory, just as Marshall Sahlins describes the negotiation of western capitalism by indigenous peoples as the indigenisation of modernity (Sahlins and Kirch, 1992). To speak in this way about the interaction between indigenous people and theory avoids rendering invisible the agency of Aboriginal people.

## Migrancy, nationalism and literature

As a middle-class and Anglo-Celtic woman I am implicated by my own class and ethnic positioning in the colonising and assimilationist territorialisation of knowledges produced by minority constituencies. It is appropriate, therefore, that self-reflexivity and an 'unlearning of privilege' form the basis of my pedagogy and knowledge production. My own position in the academy, whose nationalist and patriarchal discourses either marginalise or appropriate minority constituencies' knowledges, is both interventionary and deconstructive. To this end, I focus here on the literatures of Aboriginal and ethnic minority peoples, and their interpellation into national cultures. The ethnic minority literature I focus on is represented by the writings of Ania Walwicz in Australia (Chapter 4), Philip Jeyaretnam in Singapore (Chapter 5) and Bharati Mukherjee in the

USA (Chapter 6). In order to avoid reducing my discussion of these texts to an exercise in aesthetics it is necessary to examine the cultural situations of these writers and their work.

In discussing Ania Walwicz's writings in the context of multiculturalism, for example, I examine her specific interpellation or positioning as an ethnicised subject in Australia. Various Poles have argued that the entry into Anglo-Celtic Australian culture has been less conflictual for Poles than for some other ethnic groups. The history of Australia's immigrant intake has been sculpted by a sense of which ethnic groups have been seen as desirable at various times. The founding of Federation in 1901 was also a moment of the articulation of race, for among the first pieces of legislation formulated by the new Federal Parliament was the Immigration Restriction Act, which implemented the so-called White Australia Policy (Kalantzis and Cope, 1993:121). After the introduction of the mass-migration programme of 1947, the first influx of migrants comprised Baltic and Slav people who were considered not only anti-Communist but also 'racially acceptable' and therefore more readily assimilable. This was followed by an influx of southern Europeans, such that by the 1950s the largest sources of migrants were Italy, Greece and Malta (Castles and Miller, 1993:74). Non-Europeans were not admitted at this stage. The White Australia Policy remained in force until the Federal Labor Conference of 1965 when references to it were dropped (Foster and Stockley, 1984:54). Although the post-war years 1947–51 saw the greatest influx of Poles, Polish political and economic refugees and immigrants continued to arrive in the following decades, particularly after the political upheavals in Poland in 1956, 1968 and 1980–81 (Sussex and Zubrzycki, 1985:4). Ania Walwicz migrated to Australia with her family in 1963 at the age of twelve.

Jock Collins has argued that northern Europeans were most successful at assimilating to the system, and that by the 1970s the new Australian 'middle' class was disproportionately northern European. These were the immigrants most likely to be in administrative jobs, and they had a greater presence in the corporate 'ruling' class (Collins, 1984:16–17). Sussex and Zubrzycki observe that Poles in Australia have escaped 'ethnic animosity', and that 'if there is a distinction between acceptable and suspicious Europeans, then the Poles are acceptable' (Sussex and Zubrzycki, 1985:1). They describe Poles as a 'quiet presence' (ibid.:6) in Australia, which suggests that they have assimilated to Anglo-Celtic Australian culture. Ania Walwicz confirms the relative lack of racism here towards Poles (n.d.[b]:7). The situation would appear to be similar in other western cultures; Stephen Steinberg, for example, describes Poles in the USA as 'white ethnics' (Steinberg, 1981:3). In assimilating more easily than some other ethnicities, Poles can thus be seen as having contributed to the 'internationalisation of the Australian ruling class' (Collins, 1984:18).

Chapter 4 surveys Ania Walwicz's three books, *writing* (1982), *boat* (1989) and *red roses* (1992), as well as sundry other pieces. It also undertakes a detailed reading of *red roses*. I argue that the trajectory of Ania Walwicz's diaspora and immigration—and the role that forgetting, memory and history play in the reconstruction of that trajectory—are determined by her specific Polish immigrant background and her relationship with the nationalist discourse of Australian literature. In spite of her interest in avant-garde forms, Walwicz eschews 'radical ideology' (Walwicz, 1992b:835), and expresses her desire to be accepted into mainstream publishing and the Australian canon. This ambition is well realised; her work is represented in over fifty anthologies (Walwicz, 1992b:835), she has won the Victorian Premier's Literary Award and the ANZ New Writing Award, various writer-in-residency appointments, major literary grants, and her texts are studied in schools and universities.

In his discussion of diasporic literatures (and in particular Polish diasporic narratives) Vijay Mishra observes that

> diasporas which have more readily become part of the assimila-tionist narrative of the nation-state (like the Poles, Italians and Armenians in the US, and in other settler societies such as Australia and Canada) do not have the same need to construct myths of homelands for ethnopolitical or coalitional mobilisations. (Mishra, 1994:4)

However, he goes on to comment that formulations of theories of diaspora and the homeland need to be 'supplemented by . . . divergent narratives of individual diasporas that spell out, within the general parameters of a set of diasporic universals, quite specific versions of the diasporic imaginary' (ibid.). Even if Ania Walwicz has no apparent 'ethnopolitical or coalitional' aim or intent, this does not prevent our seeing her work as belonging to a series of diasporic narratives, and as such it narrates a specific and ethnicised subject-position. Walwicz constructs both a particular history of migration and a particular myth of the homeland; her Polish ethnicity, moreover, is further articulated by a narrative of Jewish diaspora. If her work can be read as having a political effect—and I suggest that her formal radicalism is inevitably political—it is to rewrite and globalise the nationalist discourse of multiculturalism.

The construction of ethnicity by nationalist discourse is based upon a belief in the separateness of different cultures, each of which is bounded and reified. But in fact the culture of any group is dynamic, and changes as it is redefined by each generation. Against the culturalism of multiculturalism, therefore, I argue for a postmodern and performative ethnicity, that is, an ethnicity that comes into being through the enactment of strategies and positions. Reservations have been expressed about using the lexicon of postmodernity in the context of ethnicity and diaspora (e.g. Perera, 1993). I aim to avoid, however, both the aestheticising of migrancy (that is, the state of being a migrant) and the 'repressive tolerance' of pluralism by mapping the processes by which Ania Walwicz is interpellated as an ethnicised subject in such a way that her work can intervene in and redefine the canon of Australian literature.

Her emphasis in *red roses* on the performative nature of ethnicity and gender parodies multiculturalism's project of officially recording memory and 'museumising' ethnicity, thereby turning it into unproblematic objects of display. By foregrounding the performative aspects of body and voice, the text foregrounds both the fictionality of representation and the instability of meaning. This evokes the relativised space of the migrant, which is similarly unstable and subject to change according to the different experience and 'performance' of each generation. My discussion of *red roses* suggests that Australian literature is characterised as much by cosmopolitan as by national formations, and that figurations of migrancy are as typical of Australian culture as are representations of national situatedness. Walwicz's entry into the Australian literary canon represents an internationalisation of it. Her affiliation with the European avant-garde and exploration of her own European 'heritage' (Walwicz, n.d.[b]:11) constitute a culturally specific moment of globalisation in Australian culture.

I suggest in Chapter 4 that it is useful to think of the literary canon as being reconstituted in this way, and to follow the Canadian example of formulating 'ethnicity in literature' (Gunew, 1993:453). For by doing so we can redefine what we mean by literature and Australian literature, instead of merely confirming the current regulatory discourse which marginalises 'ethnic', 'migrant' or 'multicultural' literature. As Gillian Bottomley reminds us (1992:54), texts classified as ethnic or multicultural (such as a concert of folk dances) have a minority status compared to texts that are defined as 'high' culture (such as a Mozart concert).

Australia has been described as one of the 'classical countries of immigration', a new nation formed by colonisation and migration over the last two centuries. In 1991 about 23 per cent of its total population had been born overseas, and about 20 per cent of those born in Australia had at least one immigrant parent; over four in every ten Australians therefore have close links with the migratory process (Castles and Miller, 1993:99). Australia is second only to Israel in the numbers and range of its migrant population (Pettman, 1992b:35). The process of making visible migrant histories and incorporating them into a general history of Australia, however, has been slow. Approximately two decades after the introduction of multicultural policy in Australia, histories of the massive immigration of non-Anglophone people, for example, are relegated to the field of studies of migrants, ethnics and multicultural studies (Bottomley, 1992:145). By incorporating texts such as Ania Walwicz's into the canon of Australian literature—and in the process main-taining rather than eliding their historical and cultural specificities —the canon is remade and globalised. The recognition of the processes of diaspora and migration as central to the formation of Australia may enable us to develop, in Spivak's words, a 'trans-national literacy' appropriate to a country shaped by immigration (Spivak, 1992:14).

By contrast with Australia, the discourse of diaspora in the USA would appear to be more dominant than that of multiculturalism.

According to Mishra (1994:3), 'diasporic theory is what underpins multicultural theory'. This statement is valid if we consider that the term 'migrant' evokes a relationship to a nation, while 'diaspora' implies a global arena. Diasporic histories, moreover, extend to those generations born in 'host' countries, whereas the term 'migrant' refers only to the immigrant generation. I use these different terms to delineate the dual dynamics of local and global histories. For me (perhaps arbitrarily) the term 'migrant', as I have suggested, evokes a sense of negotiation within national contexts, whereas 'diasporic' suggests globally connected pasts and futures. Both terms, needless to say, represent the nation's 'other', and in Ien Ang's words 'unsettle static, essentialist and totalitarian conceptions of "national culture" or "national identity" with origins firmly rooted in fixed geography and common history' (Ang, 1993:41). A key metaphor in the American discourse of diaspora, however—and one which would appear less relevant in Australia—is that of the 'border'. In the American context, this pertains as much to geographical as cultural and psychic phenomena.

If nations are defined against their 'others', they are formed by the dual processes of inclusion and exclusion, of remembering and forgetting. Colonial myths of 'discovery' ignored the histories of Aboriginal people and their experience of the violence of the colonising project. Migrant people in turn have experienced the violence of assimilation. We see evidence of such processes in the systemic exclusion of migrant histories from 'Australian' history, and the officially organised structures of forgetting in relation to Aboriginal histories. Both constituencies have been marginalised by racism, which Humphrey McQueen calls 'the most important single component of Australian nationalism' (quoted in Hodge and Mishra, 1990:180). In Ania Walwicz's work I trace a progression from a denial of the past (and the 'degradation and destruction' that the process of migration and assimilation can represent) to the assertion of difference and the affirmation both of European roots and a global identity.

In relation to both its indigenous and immigrant constituencies, mainstream Australian culture experiences periods of socially organised amnesia that repress histories of violence. As repressed memories are uncovered and articulated we become aware of how discontinuous the present is with both local and global histories. This is the hallmark of those 'new times' in which both the local and the global exist simultaneously (Hall, 1989:133). And however removed it may appear to be from local or global formations of identity, the nation is always their shadowy point of reference (I. Chambers, 1990:46). The nation is thus both continually *in the making* and continually *making* culture. By redrawing national literary maps, this book aims to expose discontinuities and to chart the voices of migrant and indigenous writers. For these tell of the omissions, silences and (in Mukherjee's case) complicities of national literary histories in the promulgation of assimilation and homogeneity.

## National and postmodern subjectivities

Despite their common experience of marginalisation, migrants and Aboriginal people do not stand in the same relation of otherness to the metropolitan centre. Post-war migration to Australia was not informed by a colonial history as was the case in the United Kingdom, for example. Australian indigenous and immigrant peoples have divergent histories; Aboriginal people resist being drawn under the umbrella of multiculturalism on account of its assimilationist implications. Instead, Aboriginal people maintain their racial difference in order to foreground the violence of their encounter with imperialism and a still largely invisible colonial history of slavery and exploitation. It is for its implicitly political critique that the term 'race' continues to be necessary (Hegeman, 1991:78). Aboriginal people avoid conflating their own political agenda—at the foreground of which are land rights and native title—with the very different ethnopolitical agendas of various 'multicultural' groups (Langford, 1994c:26; Fesl, 1993b:167). Very few links have been formed between these two constituencies in Australia; indeed, Aboriginal people have formed global pan-indigenous coalitions more readily than alliances with ethnic minority groups within Australia. Many Aboriginal people feel that because migrants have not suffered cultural domination and decimation on the same scale they are less disadvantaged. As Ruby Langford Ginibi says:

We Kooris are fifteen to twenty years behind everyone else in all the basic human rights such as health, housing, employment and education; even the people who migrate here are on a higher social level than we are, and we're the first people of this land! My people were forced to give away using our language and culture, and adopt the ways of the white man, but the people who migrated here don't give away their language or culture to become Australian citizens. (Langford, 1994b:52)

Conversely, it is claimed that the burgeoning of academic interest in the oppression of indigenous people 'produces an even greater amnesia regarding other histories, including postwar migration histories' (Gunew, 1993:449). The histories and political agendas of these two constituencies are divergent if not oppositional. This is reflected also in their different relationship to nationalism. A comparable case is the anomalous relationship of American Indians with United States nationalism. Indians are citizens both of the USA and of officially recognised 'nations' inhabiting areas designated as 'reservations', 'reserves' and 'colonies'. The existence of such areas enables American Indians to experience 'multiple nationality' (Strong and Van Winkle, 1993:9). This anomalous citizenship challenges the sovereignty of the USA and exposes the incomplete nature of national hegemony. There are some points of similarity here with the situation of Aborigines and their own claims to sovereignty and nationhood. The status of Aboriginal people as the 'first' or indigenous people—neither immigrant nor 'settler'—troubles identifications of the nation (see, for example, the essays on indigenous sovereignty in the April 1994 issue of *Social Alternatives*).

Strong and Van Winkle also describe how tribal and national identities are being supplanted by transnational identities, either pan-Indian or pan-indigene (ibid.:20). They suggest that Indians, who are 'adept at subverting hegemonic nationalist narratives and crossing national borders', and who in addition are 'familiar with multiple forms of belonging and exclusion', exemplify 'the complex form of identity that has come to be known as post-modern' (ibid.). Stuart Hall has made the same claim in relation to black people, as discussed in Chapter 4. In debates on postmodernism, the archetypal postmodern subjectivity ranges from the most marginalised of constituencies to the white Anglo-Celtic male—that privileged and universal subject who, in postmodernity, experiences the erosion of those grand narratives in which his authority is invested. Amidst this cornucopia of claims to represent postmodernity, Slippers' comic revelation in *Bran Nue Dae*—'Ich bien Ine Aborigine [sic]' (Chi and Kuckles, 1991:71)—would appear exemplary.

Nelly Richard similarly argues that the culturally hybrid Latin American periphery was postmodernist *avant la lettre* (in advance of the term). Although she qualifies her definition with the observation that 'postmodernism abolishes any privilege which such a position might offer', and that 'the center, though claiming to be in disintegration, still operates as a center' (Richard, 1987–88:10–11), she nevertheless argues that postmodernism has been enabling for the periphery because it has opened up a space for the reconsideration of 'all that was "left unsaid"' by the narratives of modernity (ibid.:12). In chapters 4 and 5 I argue that Michael Fischer's concept of a 'postmodern ethnicity' is useful because it emphasises ethnicity as a dynamic, changing formation that is as much future-oriented as dependent on the past. I use Fischer's argument in a discussion of ethnic minority writing as exemplified by Ania Walwicz and Philip Jeyaretnam. The notion of a dynamic, performative and future-oriented subjectivity is also relevant to discussions of Aboriginality in order to counter the relegation of indigenous culture to the past. Strong and Van Winkle (gesturing towards Berkhofer) argue that Native Americans 'are viewed as noble or ignoble opponents, as obstacles to progress or its victims, as objects of scorn or objects of pity—but always as belonging to the past and incompatible with the future' (Strong and Van Winkle, 1993:19). Andrew Lattas similarly points out that Aboriginal culture is constructed by the dominant discourse as encoding a spirituality lost to western civilisation, and which must be reclaimed in order to overcome non-Aboriginal Australians' 'alienation' from the land (Lattas, 1990:62).

It would appear, therefore, that postmodernism has points both of convergence with and divergence from the project of Aborigi-nality, as I argue in Chapter 3. The points of convergence I have outlined above. Among the points of divergence, I would number postmodernist claims about the disintegration of the subject, the deferral of closure, and the dispersal of meaning. We must be wary of translating the crises and anxieties of subjectivity across different constituencies. For example, the claim that 'our individual stories, our unconscious drives and desires, acquire a form that is always contingent, in transit, without a goal, without an end' (I. Chambers, 1994:25) is not supported by Aboriginal women's autobiographical narratives which have an avowed political agenda and a clearly stated goal. This is not to deny, however, that the construction of Aboriginality is itself 'contingent' and 'in transit', or that it will undergo changes in response to changing political contexts. But Aboriginal texts will always have a 'goal', even if simply as a counter-discourse to the dominant discourse of Australian nationalism (Trees, 1992). And as I have suggested, Aboriginal memory is very different from what is generally described as postmodern memory.

## Post-colonialism and Aboriginal literature

Although post-colonialism can be useful when describing certain aspects of post-invasion culture in Australia (such as the relationship between Australia and the United Kingdom or the west), as a discourse it has not been scrupulous in distinguishing between the very different formations of colonisation and decolonisation in 'settler' and indigenous cultures. In Aboriginal contexts the term 'post-colonial' has limited currency, and in smaller *récits* (narratives) may never be used (Mishra and Hodge, 1991:412). This may be the case also in other 'post-colonial' and 'settler' ('invasion') contexts, where post-coloniality is a condition but not a political strategy in the way that anti-colonial and decolonising movements are. The latter, in their rhetoric of revolution, imply a break or severance from colonisation. The discourse of post-colonialism, on the other hand, may well imply a continuing relationship and complicity with various forms of colonisation.

My own introduction to Aboriginal literature was through my interests in post-colonial studies and feminism, and was further facilitated serendipitously through my moving to the west coast. It did not take me long to realise that the discourses of post-colonialism and feminism diverged from that of Aboriginality. Radically re-thinking both my feminism and my concept of post-colonialism, it soon became apparent to me that 'post-colonialism' was unsatisfactory as a general term. Like Ella Shohat (1992:99) I would argue for a more limited use of the term, theoretically and historically specific, and mobilised in the service of small rather than grand *récits*, and in the context of Anglo-Celtic Australian rather than Aboriginal culture. Aboriginal people do not produce narratives of post-coloniality or even decolonisation, although in their demand for self-determination they certainly articulate what Ngugi (1986) calls 'decolonising the mind'. (For a fuller discussion of self-determination, see Mick Dodson, 1994:68.) What they write and speak are narratives of continuing dispossession and surveillance. As Marcia Langton points out, the decolonisation of institutions and Anglo-Celtic culture in general is ultimately an impossible and utopian goal. More immediate tasks are the project of undermining cultural hegemony and the critique of such forms of neo-colonialism as welfare colonialism (Langton, 1993:8). I argue in Chapter 3 that Aboriginal literature cannot be described as post-colonial while Aboriginal people are still living in conditions of colonisation in what is described euphemistically as a 'settler' culture. As Ruby Langford Ginibi makes clear,

> we are invaded people, and have been since 1788 . . . We have always had to conform to the laws and standards of the invaders. Our tribal laws mean nothing to the white man, our traditional people were classified as heathens and vermin to be cleared off the face of the earth. Assimilate us or wipe us out was the order of the day. (Langford, 1994b:51–2)

Comparing the situation here with that in New Zealand, where the Maori population is bigger, Simon During has observed that Australia, as a nation comprising both Aboriginal and non-Aboriginal people, has 'almost no possibility of entry into the post-colonised condition' (During, 1987:45). Whether, in fact, indigenous sovereignty will eventuate in Australia (as it has, for example, in the USA), and whether that would confer a post-colonial status upon Aboriginal people, are open questions. During later modified his pessimism when conceding that, with recognition of the illegitimacy of the nation's origins, 'a genuinely postcolonial Australia is at last imaginable'. A condition of this form of post-coloniality would be the nation's admission to itself of the limits of its own legitimacy, and the grounding of nationhood in the memory of those indigenous people destroyed in the establishment of the colonial state (During, 1992:353).

## Post-colonialism, nationalism, globalism

Notions of what is post-colonial vary between Australia and the USA. In Australia the texts examined under the rubric of post-colonial studies are mostly written in English by people from countries formerly colonised by Britain. Post-colonial literary studies in Australia are epitomised by *The Empire Writes Back* (1989), an ambitious book that attempts to provide the framework of a post-colonial reading practice applicable to any culture which is now beyond its specifically colonial period. Bill Ashcroft, Gareth Griffiths and Helen Tiffin define post-colonial texts as those which 'interrogate and subvert imperial formations' through the tactics of abrogation and appropriation:

> Abrogation is a refusal of the categories of the imperial culture, its aesthetic, its illusory standard of normative or 'correct' usage, and its assumption of a traditional and fixed meaning 'inscribed' in the words. It is a vital moment in the de-colonising of the language and the writing of 'english', but without the process of appropriation the moment of abrogation may not extend beyond a reversal of the assumptions of privilege, the 'normal', and correct inscription, all of which can be simply taken over and maintained by the new usage. (Ashcroft et al., 1989:38)

Quoting Diana Brydon, they argue that studies of the 'silenced and marginalised' post-colonial voice—and of its 'decentering' and difference—anticipated the interest shown by post-structuralism and postmodernism in cultural relativity and the subversive power of the marginal (ibid.:12, 139). More recently, Homi Bhabha has reiterated this position. He suggests that 'the encounters and negotiations of differential meanings and values within "colonial" textuality' have anticipated, *avant la lettre*, the issues of contemporary theory (Bhabha, 1994:173). His own project, accordingly, is to 'rename the postmodern from the position of the postcolonial' (ibid.:175).

There is no doubt that post-colonial literary studies in Australia during the 1970s and 1980s challenged the notion of 'a single culture masquerading as the originating centre' (Ashcroft et al., 1989:196), exposed the literary canon's repressed relationship to otherness, and introduced non-Anglo-Celtic texts into school and university syllabi. In focusing on the specificities of British colonisation, however, post-colonial studies overlooked the global reconfiguration of power, and in particular the part played by multinational and transnational corporations from the 1960s onwards in reinscribing economic and cultural domination. The modernisation and 'development' of Third World countries—facilitated by the international monetary system and the World Bank—inflicted upon those countries (in Susan George's words) 'a fate worse than debt' (quoted in McClintock, 1992:95). As McClintock suggests, 'despite the hauling down of colonial flags in the 1950s, revamped economic imperialism has ensured that America and the former European colonial powers have become richer, while, with a tiny scattering of exceptions, their ex-colonies have become poorer' (ibid.:94).

The liberatory and emancipatory rhetoric of post-colonialism seems out of place in this context. This is not to suggest that resistance is not viable, but rather that it needs to be theorised in much more subtle and nuanced ways. Moreover, because post-colonialism has developed unevenly across the globe, historically specific discussions—small *récits* rather than grand narratives—are necessary in order to avoid subsuming difference in a pluralist model. Several reviewers of *The Empire Writes Back*, for example, raise the problem of imposing the one theoretical model on different cultural terrains (e.g. Sharrad, 1990). And Henry Louis Gates, in critiquing the ascendance of the colonial paradigm, poses a similar question: 'do we still need global, imperial theory—in this case, a grand unified theory of oppression?' (Gates, 1991:470).

In fact, the notion of the post-colonial has only a limited circulation globally. It has little currency in African, Middle Eastern and Latin American intellectual circles, except in the restricted historical sense of naming the period immediately after the end of colonial rule (Shohat, 1992:106). Kwame Anthony Appiah would agree with this description for Africa. Post-coloniality, he believes, is the condition of 'a relatively small, Western-style, Western trained group of writers and thinkers, who mediate the trade in cultural commodities of world capitalism at the periphery', and who are dependent for their support on the existence of African universities and Euro-American publishers and readers (Appiah, 1991:348). In the context of Australian culture, the notion of post-colonialism is narrowing. The post-war immigrant population, for example, does not share the Anglo-Celtic experience of post-colonialism, partly because its 'homelands' are diverse, and partly because there is no simple way in which Aboriginal culture can be described as post-colonial.

Australian post-colonial literary studies have tended not to examine either the neo-colonial reconfiguration of the globe or the place of English-speaking elites in post-colonial countries as well as in the First World. By contrast, American studies of post-colonialism have focused on such notions as global flows, migrancy, diaspora and transnationality, particularly with respect to diasporic intellectuals living in the USA. That diasporic and English-speaking elite represents 'the heritage of imperialism in the rest of the globe' (Spivak, 1993:280).

Transformations within the world capitalist economy, and the growth of both multinational corporations during the 1960s and transnational corporations since the mid 1970s (Miyoshi, 1993), have resulted in the emergence of what is variously called 'post-industrial global culture', 'disorganised capital' or 'late capitalism'. Arjun Appadurai (1990) describes five types of global flows:

- ethnoscapes, or the landscape of people who constitute the shifting world (tourists, immigrants, refugees, exiles, guestworkers, etc.)
- mediascapes, or the flow of images and narratives enabled by electronic technologies
- technoscapes, or the global configuration of mechanical and informational technology across previously impervious boundaries
- finanscapes, or the global movement of capital
- ideoscapes, or the global transportability of ideologies and concepts such as 'freedom', 'sovereignty', 'democracy', 'nation', etc.

Some theorists argue that the nation is in decline with the rise of global cultures. (It is important to note here that 'globalisation' results not in one singular, homogenous global culture, but many global cultures.) 'Against the effective operation of TNCs [transnational corporations]', writes Masao Miyoshi (1993:743), 'the nation-states more and more look undefined and inoperable'. He argues that the nation-state is a 'nostalgic and sentimental myth that offers an illusion of a classless organic community', and that in the functions it is supposed to perform (such as protecting public health, providing general education, maintaining security, and guiding national economy) it is a failure (ibid.:744).

Although the nation may well seem an anachronism, it nevertheless survives. Hans Kohn observed in 1971 that nationalism had become the most widespread political discourse since World War II. In the three decades after the end of that war, more than ninety new nations emerged as the result of independence movements and the renegotiation of borders (Schiller, 1976:39). This included a number of Islamic nations such as Libya, Egypt, Saudi Arabia, Jordan, Syria, Iraq, Pakistan and Indonesia (in the first two decades of this century there had been only three Islamic states: Turkey, Persia and Afghanistan [Kohn, 1971:83]). The list also includes South and South-east Asian post-colonial nations such as India, the Philippines, Sri Lanka, Cambodia, Laos and Burma (Myanmar), and later Malaysia, Singapore and Vietnam. The establishment of post-colonial nations continued into the 1970s in Africa after the withdrawal of British, French, Belgian and Portuguese colonial powers.

Nationalism is usually considered to be of European and, specifically, English origin (ibid.:16). Yet according to Benedict Anderson (1991), it first appeared in Spanish America between 1760 and 1830 as a result of Creole anti-metropolitan feeling and resentment of the imperial centre. Anderson describes the European nationalisms which developed in the period 1815–50 as 'second-generation' nationalist movements which pirated the South American model. Other historians and post-colonial theorists, such as Gayatri Spivak, claim that concepts like 'nationhood', 'citizenship', 'constitutionality', and 'sovereignty'—all of which have political efficacy in decolonisation movements—were in fact coded within the legacy of imperialism, and borrowed by post-colonial nations from western Europe. These concepts, she believes, function catachrestically, that is, 'as concept-metaphors for which no historically adequate referent may be advanced from postcolonial space' (Spivak, 1990b:225).

Segal and Handler (1992) may be said to negotiate the space between Anderson and Spivak. They argue that the concept of nations as bounded and individuated units—and the retrojection of such units into the past in search of origins—needs to be defamiliarised and examined anew. They suggest instead that nationalisms arose as a result of the ordering of power relations both within and beyond Europe's boundaries. Nationalism, like modernity, has a colonial genealogy, and 'did not originate solely, or even primarily in "Europe". Rather', they argue, 'it emerged from globally dispersed interactions in which European, national selves and raced, but not nationed, Others were mutually constituted' (Segal and Handler, 1992:12). The European concept of the nation and the national self was thus defined against that of the colonised other. In this reading of the nation, consequently, we can rediscover the inscription of the colonised in those histories they have been written out of. I have suggested that Paul Gilroy argues a similar point in relation to the peoples of the 'black Atlantic', and Aboriginal people have reminded us that the rural industries in Australia were founded on Aboriginal labour.

Jean Franco has written about the role of nationalism in post-colonial contexts. Like Frantz Fanon (1968) she critiques the bourgeois elite. She argues that in Latin America the nation states were 'vehicles for (often enforced) capitalist modernisation . . . [which] occurred for the most part without grass-roots participation of any form of democratic debate and was often vehiculated by autocratic or populist/authoritarian regimes' (Franco, 1989:205). Suggesting that in contemporary Latin American culture the status of nationalism is ambiguous, she points to 'the simultaneous dissolution of the idea of the nation and the continuous persistence of national concerns' (ibid.:211).

This persistence of nationalism is striking in the age of global culture. In Chapter 5 I look at how two Singaporean writers, Arthur Yap and Philip Jeyaretnam, rewrite official discourses of nationalism by drawing on a vernacular and informal sense of history and the subjectivity of everyday life. In Chapter 6 I examine the work of Bharati Mukherjee and her acclamation of American nationalism. In both her fictional and non-fictional writing she reinvents and redefines nationalism in terms of the 'gutsy' spirit of immigrants and their ability to transmogrify and take on new identities. She hails the migrant as the 'new pioneer', a 'conqueror' and a 'hero'. I argue that in her romance of the USA as the new world of opportunity she disavows the class context of her own privileged entry into the USA.

This argument accords to some extent with the recent critique of post-colonialism by Arif Dirlik (1994). Like most North American theorists, he identifies the post-colonial with Third World intellectuals in the First World, prominent among whom are post-colonials of Indian origin. He goes on to argue that post-coloniality is the condition of the intelligentsia in global capitalism, and that the relationship between post-colonialism and global capital pertains not only to cultural and epistemological but also to social and political formations. He suggests that the incorporation of these formerly marginal voices into the centre means that post-colonial discourse is an expression of newly found power, and that post-colonials disguise and disavow their relationship with global capitalism. Post-colonialism needs to generate, therefore, a critique of its own ideology.

Dirlik's discussion of how post-colonial intellectuals disavow their origins in a global capitalism of which they are 'not so much victims as beneficiaries' (Dirlik, 1994:353) impinges on my own critique of Mukherjee. Inflecting Dirlik's argument somewhat, I examine how transnationality is enabled by post-coloniality, and the role played by transnationality and cosmopolitanism in the contemporary reinvention of American nationalism. In exploring the possibility of other positions that diasporic post-colonials might adopt *vis-à-vis* their interpellation into the First World, I use the work of Gayatri Spivak. A Bengali of similar social origins to Mukherjee, Spivak (like her) emigrated to North America in the early 1960s. She adopts a deconstructive strategy in order to critique the post-imperialist structure that the post-colonial 'inhabits intimately' (Spivak, 1993:281).

The formations of post-colonialism, nationalism and globalism bear on the following chapters which explore on the one hand issues of migrancy, transnationality and homelands in the work of minority ethnic writers and, on the other hand, the decolonising projects and contestatory or oppositional subjectivity of Aboriginal people. Questions of agency, resistance, counter-discursivity, self-determination, the assertion of difference and the reclaiming of histories impinge upon both ethnic minority and indigenous constituencies. As I have suggested, the decolonising, the reclaiming and the rewriting of previously invisible histories bring about a refiguring of identity not only for these marginalised constituencies but also for the dominant cultural groups. This book itself results from a rethinking of my own knowledge of the 'other', and of how other knowledges might intervene in the constraining and enabling formations of post-colonialism, nationalism and globalism.

# 2

# Reading Aboriginal Women's Autobiographical Narratives: The Repressive Hypothesis

In this chapter I examine Stephen Muecke's application of Michel Foucault's discussion of the repressive hypothesis to two auto-biographical narratives published within a year of each other: Sally Morgan's *My Place* (1987) and Glenyse Ward's *Wandering Girl* (1988). In his discussion of the repressive hypothesis, Foucault questions whether the relationship between power, knowledge and sexuality (for which we can substitute the term 'Aboriginal literature') can in fact be defined in terms of repression (Foucault, 1984:6–13). According to Muecke, the repressive hypothesis impinges upon the discourse of Aboriginal literature in two ways. First, it has been mobilised 'as an explanatory account of the emergence of Aboriginal literature'; secondly, it 'works at the individual level as a technique for the psychological construction of a specific sort of Aboriginal subject . . . [i.e.] the autobiographical attempt to inscribe a politics of Aboriginal coming-to-consciousness' (Muecke, 1988:408).

In his first application of the repressive hypothesis, Muecke characterises the development of Aboriginal literature. 'The story of Aboriginal relations to the publishing industry', he points out, 'is not one of persecution and struggle as the repressive hypothesis might lead us to believe'. On the contrary, the publishing industry has been 'in a state of readiness, even eagerness, to publish work by Aboriginal writers' (ibid.:412–13). 'Aboriginality', he continues, 'is a social "truth" which must be uttered' (ibid.:413), that is, at the prompting of white Australians. 'The meanings of *Wandering Girl* and *My Place*', he suggests, 'are over- or pre-determined by a social formation which demands that Aboriginal issues be spoken in the name of social justice' (ibid.:416). *My Place*, Muecke contends, is mediated by a 'whole series of well meaning whites bringing us the book' (ibid.). And among those whites are reviewers who tell a predominantly Anglo-Celtic reading public that they 'should take up the burden of guilt for the wrongs of the past' (ibid.).

In constructing these Aboriginal narratives as products solely of white technologies (that is, of a complex of social and cultural practices such as institutional and popularised discourses and epistemologies through which the dominant culture fashions notions of racial identity), Muecke is in danger of writing out the agency of Aboriginal people. His analysis, moreover, homogenises the various subject-positions that *My Place* offers its readership. There are, of course, reviewers who stress the issue of white Australian guilt, such as Daniel (1988) and Gare (1987), but theirs is not necessarily the only or the most representative reading of the book. At the heart of Muecke's critique is an anxiety about guilt. Guilt, however, is not the only economy of desire possible for a white Australian who reads Aboriginal texts, although it is commonly invoked by the New Right, for example, as a counter-discourse to Aboriginal reforms (Keeffe, 1992:155–8).

Feminists working in the area of minority literatures have explored the issue of white women's guilt. The black lesbian Audre Lorde and the Indian-American Chandra Mohanty (in collaboration with Biddy Martin) both have investigated how white women react to the writings of minority women. Martin and Mohanty (in a discussion of Minnie Bruce Pratt's autobiography) suggest that guilt traps whites 'within the boundaries of a coherent "white" identity', and thus produces paralysis and defensiveness (Martin and Mohanty, 1986:198). Borrowing Pratt's phrase, 'cultural impersonation', they define it as 'a tendency among white women to respond with guilt and self-denial to the knowledge of racism . . . and to borrow or take on the identity of the Other in order to avoid not only guilt but pain and self-hatred' (ibid.:207). Lorde similarly suggests that 'guilt is only another form of objectification', a response to one's own actions or lack of action. If it leads to change then it can be useful, since it is then no longer guilt but the beginning of knowledge. Yet all too often, guilt is just another name for impotence, for defensiveness destructive of communication; it becomes a device to protect ignorance and the continuation of things the way they are, the ultimate protection for changeless-ness. (Lorde, 1984b:132, 130)

What Lorde and Martin and Mohanty point to, then, are other reading positions for whites in relation to minority texts. Aboriginal people have also emphasised the need for white Australians to move beyond their guilt as it prevents them developing a new understanding of Aboriginal people. Ruby Langford, for example, states: 'perhaps one day we will receive the recognition we truly deserve when white Australia overcomes all their guilty feelings about us' (Langford, 1994c:135). Noel Pearson similarly observes that 'it is those who refuse to recognise and acknowledge the past who are most troubled by guilt. Only with acknowledgement can the debilitating baggage of our past be dispensed with' (Pearson, 1994:3).

Muecke also uses Foucault's repressive hypothesis in his critique of the construction of speaking subjects in *My Place* and *Wandering Girl*. He suggests that Aboriginal subjectivity in these texts is constructed through the 'expression' of the self. The self is realised, as it were, purely through the means of expression, outside and beyond any social influence. This notion of subjectivity, Muecke suggests, invokes 'the fullness and primacy of the voice', which is held to be a source of 'original or creative material' (Muecke, 1988:406). He describes Morgan's and Ward's autobiographical narratives as enacting the 'technology of the ethical self' (ibid.:411). Borrowing further from Foucault, Muecke suggests that the mode of narration or 'autobiographical style' (ibid.:409) of these books is confessional. It is a discourse whose purpose is 'the production of truth' or 'notions of truth' (ibid.:416). Here Muecke quotes Foucault: '"one goes about telling, with the greatest precision, whatever is most difficult to tell"' (ibid.:410). The 'confessional discourse' of *My Place* is enabled by 'a liberationist politics' (ibid.): through expressing the self, liberation from silence and oppression is achieved. The 'liberatory romance' (ibid.:407) of these auto-biographies is that to 'confess' or 'express oneself' is to be free.

## Self versus society

In his critique of Ward's and Morgan's autobiographical narratives Muecke evokes two dichotomies. The first is that of self and society: he characterises this opposition as the individual versus the collective—'the primacy of the individual set against its contradictory term, human collectivity' (ibid.:409). Morgan and Ward's auto-biographical project, according to Muecke, is one of 'radical individualism' (ibid.:411), whereby the writer is concerned with personal salvation and redemption: the isolated (Aboriginal) individual struggles against and finally transcends a hostile (white) society. Society (or 'human collectivity' in Muecke's phrase) is imaged only inasmuch as it is antagonistic to the protagonist's progress. The 'romance of liberation' constructed by the 'confessional' discourse of these Aboriginal women's autobiographies positions 'the social/political sphere as the negative side of free self-expression' (ibid.:418). In *Writing from the Fringe* (1990) Mudrooroo puts forward a similar argument, although he approaches the topic of community from a different perspective. Like Muecke he proposes that the narrative of *My Place* is alienated from the community, but in this case from the Aboriginal community. He describes *My Place* as 'an individualised story [where] the concerns of the Aboriginal community are of secondary importance' (Narogin, 1990:149). (He does however later shift his position on *My Place*; see Mudrooroo, 1992.)

This apparent dichotomy between self and society can be critiqued by means of feminist and minority discourse theories. A large body of writing by feminists on women's autobiography (and particularly on the autobiographies of minority and indigenous women) treats the notion of subjectivity or the self quite differently from the way it is handled in traditional, male-centred or andro-centric discourse. The histories constructed by women's autobiography, they argue, are not so much personal and individual as collective and cultural (Friedman, 1988; Reagon, 1982). In other words, the writer's individual experience is read by these feminists as representative rather than unique. A communal female identity or positionality is often further distinguished by specific racial, ethnic or cultural experience (such as being black, Aboriginal, working-class, feminist, lesbian). Most feminist studies of auto-biography emphasise the role of community and family bonds in women's lives; largely absent by comparison is the notion of the individual being, liberated from social oppression into a rarefied space of individuality. 'Without community', writes Audre Lorde (1984a:112), 'there is no liberation, only the most vulnerable and temporary armistice between an individual and her oppression'. That Sally Morgan sees herself as part of a collective—and her own story as intimately and inextricably linked to family and community —is shown by her inclusion (as parallel to her own) of the stories of her mother, grandmother and great uncle, which together comprise over a third of her book.

Minority-discourse analysis has many points of congruence or agreement with feminist theory. According to Gilles Deleuze and Felix Guattari, minority literature is inherently political and has collective value. 'Every individual matter is immediately plugged into the political', they claim, and is 'positively charged with the role and the function of collective' (Deleuze and Guattari, 1983:16, 17). Stephen Butterfield further argues that

> The self of black autobiography . . . is not an individual with a private career, but a soldier in a long, historic march towards Canaan. The self is conceived as a member of an oppressed social group, with ties and responsibilities to the other members. It is a conscious political identity, drawing sustenance from the past experience of the group. (quoted in Friedman, 1988:43)

Indeed, autobiography as a genre would appear to have a special significance for minority people; Michael Fischer suggests that whereas black Americans commonly produce autobiographies, white Americans produce more biographies (Fischer, 1986:197). Rather than making abstract the notion of subjectivity, then, Anglo-Celtic middle-class academics like myself should historicise the self or subject, and examine how it is determined by the circumstances of women's and minority people's lives. We should also recognise the fact that self-creation and self-consciousness have a specific political role for such constituencies (Friedman, 1988:43).

## Autobiographical narrative versus 'traditional Aboriginal genres'

The second dichotomy Muecke sets up in his discussion of the autobiographical narratives of Ward and Morgan is the opposition between autobiography ('with its focus on the individual history') and 'traditional Aboriginal genres' (Muecke, 1988:406). This dichotomy between contemporary writing and traditional texts also incorporates an opposition between Sally Morgan and her grandmother. Sally participates in a confessional discourse and tells all; her grandmother refuses to reveal the secrets of her past by speaking. In 'resisting the very form of the confessional', the grandmother represents 'traditional Aboriginality' which takes the form 'of non-disclosure in the face of the demand to speak' (ibid.:410). The implication here is that in speaking—in constructing her own and her families' life stories—Morgan is complicitous with white institutions, and thus represents a contaminated or 'inauthentic' Aboriginality.

Eric Michaels invokes the same dichotomy in order to level at Morgan the charge of a spurious claim to Aboriginality. He contrasts Morgan's autobiographical self (and its stress on 'personhood' and individuality) with 'Western desert oral traditions of story making and telling [which] have been described as something more collective and culturally restrained' (Michaels, 1988:45). Moreover, Morgan's Aboriginality is 'filtered' through Christianity and is thus rendered questionable. Her bogus claims to Aboriginality are exposed by comparison with those true exponents of Aboriginality, 'the elders':

> [Morgan] makes the discovery (not the invention) of an authentic, lineally-descended Aboriginal identity. What she uncovers nonetheless is so inconsistent with what we have hitherto understood about Aboriginal theologies that if Morgan is right, much will have to be rewritten and certain practising elders will have to be corrected. (ibid.)

Non-Aboriginal readers would do well at this point, as an antidote to nostalgia for a 'pure' or traditional Aboriginality, to recall Kateryna Arthur's dictum that 'the past is not infinitely repeatable and recoverable "as it was". It is remade in every telling' (Arthur, 1990:25).

The main point of my argument is that all such tendencies to dichotomise elide other reading and writing subject-positions. They situate Morgan as an Aboriginal writer who, in the face of 'traditional Aboriginality', is revealed to be at best a failure in her pale imitation of Aboriginality or, at worst, an imposter or a traitor. In such readings, *My Place* is always measured by the yardstick of an allegedly authentic Aboriginality and found lacking. Furthermore, the dichotomy Muecke constructs reads the narrative solely in racial terms. Moreover, racial identity is often overlaid by the romance of the working class 'battler'. An identification with middle-class values often disqualifies Aboriginal writers as authentic; Sally Morgan, for example, is often seen as a site of ambiguous or contentious Aboriginality on account of her middle-class interests and education (despite the fact that she grew up in a working-class family); (see, for example, Attwood, 1992).

## Genre and gender

I suggest that there are positions other than that which identifies Aboriginality in terms of race from which to read these narratives. They can be read along the axis not only of race but also of gender. It is well documented that women often read autobiography with a sense of collective or communal identity (Felski, 1989). In theorising Aboriginal women's autobiographical narratives—a bibliography of which has been compiled by Hooton (1990:392)— the gender politics of the genre need to be taken into account. I have outlined briefly above the kinds of arguments that some feminists mobilise in discussing the genre, namely notions of collectivity and the empowering politics of identity. A dichotomising reading strategy that poses an opposition between (on the one hand) complicitous, urban middle-class, and 'successful' Aboriginal people, and on the other hand those who are 'traditional' (and by implication 'elderly' and 'rural') is too limiting, for it admits only a linear and two-dimensional interpretation of these texts. In fact, many different intersections of subjectivities—of race, class and gender—are to be found there. In other words, non-Aboriginal readers should be aware of the social contexts of genre. Because many of the narrators of Aboriginal women's autobiographical narratives construct themselves primarily as mothers (or, as in Sally Morgan's case, a daughter and granddaughter), their narratives are gendered.

## Social text versus literary aesthetic

In the course of Muecke's argument a fundamental contradiction appears, namely the conflict between his desire on the one hand to treat literary texts as wholly social (that is, mobilised by the social formations that produce and circulate them), and his invocation on the other hand of a literary aesthetic. This contradiction surfaces most clearly when Muecke wants to insist that *My Place* is consti-tuted as a text by the discourse of criticism, a white discourse informed by notions of social justice and white guilt. At this point there is a slippage in his argument, especially when he goes on to lament the critical consequences of white feelings of guilt and unease about racism. 'These two books . . . can walk past the border guards of the literary institutions with Aboriginal passports', he claims, because 'who would dare say the books are bad?' (Muecke, 1988:416). Borrowing a phrase from Eric Michaels, he points to 'a lack of evaluation procedures' (ibid.) in relation to Aboriginal literature. The question here, of course, is by what standard or criteria should such evaluation be conducted.

The aesthetic 'evaluation' of Aboriginal women's autobiographical narratives has prompted some commentators to label them 'popular' as distinct from highbrow. Mudrooroo reports that some of his students think that *Wandering Girl* and *My Place* have more in common with Mills and Boon novels and gothic romances than with a resistant Aboriginality (Narogin, 1990:33). Similarly, Eric Michaels suggests that *My Place* is more akin to the television mini-series *Women of the Sun* and 'New Age astrology' than to ethnog-raphy (Michaels, 1988:45). Such comparisons betray an assessment that these women's writing is too 'personal' or 'confessional'. Although Muecke uses the term 'confessional' in the Foucauldian sense, his evaluation of *My Place* nevertheless evokes something of that more common and derogatory usage which Joanna Russ thinks trivialises women's experience (Russ, 1983:29–30). Muecke is also suspicious of the fact that *My Place* has been a best-seller, since that indicates how 'comfortably' the book has been read. 'This ease of acceptance', he explains, 'can only make the radical critic uneasy' (Muecke, 1988:415). Suspicion of the popular, however, is a common reaction to best-selling books that women read. We could well ask ourselves whether a radical practice should necessarily be suspicious of popular culture.

Both Michaels and Muecke are uncomfortable with the autobiographical aspects of *Wandering Girl* and *My Place*, partly because such books endorse the individual, and partly on account of the claims to truth made in this kind of narrative. As reasons for his discomfort, Muecke isolates the 'quasi-documentary or historical truth-effects' of the genre, its 'quasi-ethnographic realism' (ibid.:409). He objects to *Wandering Girl*'s 'franchise on absolute truth', and suggests that 'autobiographical novels with such strong claims to truth make the work of the critic difficult' (ibid.:413). Michaels complains that Morgan positions her text in such a way that 'no authority may supersede the autobiographical expert': she 'constructs criteria for evidence, history and truth which are self-referential' (Michaels, 1988:44, 45). It is because of their privileged status as the racially oppressed, he continues, that Aboriginal writers do not have to submit to conventional standards of literary judgement, but instead are invested with a kind of hallowed sanctity, motivated by the pious belief that 'Aborigines do not forget, do not lie, do not selectively interpret their memories, and so their stories are true' (ibid.:44).

Issues of truth and authenticity, however, don't have to be so daunting. They can be seen as socially specific and politically strategic rather than as epistemologically problematic. Feminists working on oral narratives are able to use the notion of truth in a less absolute way. An American group investigating women's life histories, the Personal Narratives Group, for example, proposes a different theory of reading based on the understanding that when talking about their lives, people lie sometimes, forget a lot, exaggerate, become confused, and get things wrong. Yet they *are* revealing truths. These truths don't reveal the past 'as it actually was', aspiring to a standard of objectivity. They give us instead the truths of our experiences. They aren't the result of empirical research or the logic of mathematical deductions. Unlike the reassuring Truth of the scientific ideal, the truths of personal narratives are neither open to proof nor self-evident. We come to understand them only through interpretation, paying careful attention to the contexts that shape their creation and to the world views that inform them. Sometimes the truths we see in personal narratives jar us from our complacent security as interpreters 'outside' the story and make us aware that our own place in the world plays a part in our interpretation and shapes the meanings we derive from them. (Personal Narratives Group, 1989:261)

The issue of 'truth' in Aboriginal women's narratives is not a problem of representation in general, but of who have access to representing themselves, and who in the dominant culture have a claim to 'truth'. The argument that Aboriginal people are granted access to the public sphere through publication only because of white technologies—which induce confessions from a constituency the dominant group alone has the power to name—denies Aboriginal people agency in the production of their own texts. Given that many Aboriginal women's autobiographical narratives are oral, it is necessary to examine the enunciative conditions of these texts; in the telling of Aboriginal life stories, the decision as to who tells what to whom is always a considered and inevitably a political choice. The discursive inscription of identity in Aboriginal women's narratives is thus politically strategic.

However sceptical First World critics may be about liberation narratives, the fact remains that tropes of identity and utopian spaces are common not only to women's writing but also to such con-stituencies as post-colonial, minority and indigenous peoples. A monolithic critique of identity can be destructive to those for whom creating identity is an important political project (C. West, 1989; JanMohamed and Lloyd, 1987). Those who claim impersonality or objectivity often speak from a position of privilege. Martin and Mohanty remind us of the political liabilities of an insistence on 'indeterminacy', which in fact 'denies the critic's own situatedness in the social, and in effect refuses to acknowledge the critic's own institutional home' (Martin and Mohanty, 1986:194).

# 3

# Reading Aboriginal Women's Autobiographical Narratives: Agency and Audience

I would like to explore further the issue of subjectivity as it relates to Aboriginal women's autobiographies, and specifically with respect to those strategies of agency and resistance that Aboriginal women have developed in response to past and ongoing colonisation. And I do so mindful of the fact that critiques by non-Aboriginal academics should neither disempower those strategies nor erase the issues that are important to Aboriginal people.

In a discussion of Aboriginal women's writing, Jan Larbalestier poses this question: how are minority groups' knowledges constituted? She regrets that 'Aboriginal people continue to define themselves in terms of a "black/white" opposition' (Larbalestier, 1991:91), because this dichotomous and relativistic way of thinking leads Aboriginal people to represent themselves only in relation to the dominant white culture. In using the trope of a binary opposition, Larbalestier inevitably sets up a situation of winners and losers, in which Aboriginal people are assigned to the passive and powerless 'losing' side: 'as the subordinated inheritors of the colonial condition . . . they are inevitably locked into the constraining "voice" and relentless "gaze" of the European "other"' (ibid.:77).

This is an unduly pessimistic view. I am reminded that a basic assumption of most feminist theory is that, because their experience and writing are embedded in patriarchy, women can never extricate themselves from it completely. However, they can negotiate a space from which to speak through strategies of resistance and subversion. For me, the opposition women/patriarchy will never be displaced. And, unlike Craig Owens (1985:62), I do not believe that we should try to conceive of difference without opposition. Rather than lamenting with Larbalestier the fact of opposition—that is, that Aboriginal people can define themselves only in relation to white culture—I prefer to focus on strategies of resistance in Aboriginal women's autobiographies, and to see those strategies as empowering and enabling. This is not to deny that Aboriginal literature is constrained in some measure by white discourse. But it enables us to focus productively on the agency of Aboriginal people rather than on their disarticulation.

## Women and the family: Alice Nannup and Ruby Langford Ginibi

Mudrooroo has criticised some Aboriginal women's autobiographies as assimilationist, because they do not engage directly with political issues such as land rights (Narogin, 1990:163). I would like to suggest, however, that resistance to the racist policies of the era reconstructed in these texts is not necessarily expressed in terms of overt political consciousness. Following Barry Morris's study of the Dhan-Gadi Aboriginal people in northern New South Wales, I want to isolate in these texts such tactics of resistance as the affirmation of family in the face of governmental coercion towards new forms of sociality and individuality, and the maintenance of a way of life in opposition to specific structures of domination. As Morris argues, such strategies of resistance are based on a politics of identity aimed at 'sustaining cultural distance from the dominant society which seeks their incorporation' (Morris, 1989:4).

The politics of identity in Aboriginal women's autobiography is informed by issues of race and gender (as well as class). These texts oppose not only white racism but also sexism in both Aboriginal and white culture. In raising this issue of sexism, I am fully aware that many Aboriginal women are antagonistic to western feminism which, generally speaking, has not served their interests. (I address this matter at greater length below.) Bearing in mind my earlier discussion of the universalising tendencies of white feminism, I wish neither to harness Aboriginal women writers and storytellers to any white feminist cause nor to appropriate their texts for a white feminist canon. Yet, because it is important to be vigilant about race and gender, it is worth reiterating that the inscription of self—that is, the identity politics of Aboriginal women's autobiography—is both gendered and informed by race.

The initial wave of Aboriginal life stories in the late 1950s and the 1960s focused on men. And although men have continued to produce autobiographical narratives, the genre has been dominated by women who, until the late 1980s, have been comparatively less prolific as playwrights, novelists and poets. As bibliographies by Merlan (1988) and Horton (1988) reveal, a wave of women's autobiographical and autobiographically based narratives began in the late 1970s and gained momentum a decade later with the publication of Sally Morgan's *My Place* (1987). Representative titles include Margaret Tucker's *If Everyone Cared* (1977), Monica Clare's *Karobran: The Story of an Aboriginal Girl* (1978), Ella Simon's *Through My Eyes* (1978), Shirley Smith and Bobbi (Roberta) Sykes's *Mum Shirl* (1981), Ida West's *Pride Against Prejudice* (1984), Labumore (Elsie Roughsey's) *An Aboriginal Mother Tells of the Old and the New* (1984) and Marnie Kennedy's *Born a Half-Caste* (1985). Morgan's success focused new attention on the genre; in Langford's words, 'her book was the first to open this country up' (1994a:103). As such, it represented 'a significant act of intercultural brokerage' (Donaldson, 1991:350). At that point the genre proliferated with the production of at least ten new books in the space of six years: Glenyse Ward's *Wandering Girl* (1988) and *Unna You Fullas* (1991), Ruby Langford's *Don't Take Your Love to Town* (1988), Della Walker and Tina Coutts's *Me and You* (1989), Ellie Gaffney's *Somebody Now* (1989), Patsy Cohen and Margaret Somerville's *Ingelba and the Five Black Matriarchs* (1990), Doris Pilkington's *Caprice: A Stockman's Daughter* (1991), Mabel Edmund's *No Regrets* (1992), Alice Nannup's *When the Pelican Laughed* (1992) and Evelyn Crawford's *Over My Tracks* (1993). Recently, the focus of Aboriginal women's life stories has widened to include biography and histories of the family: Sally Morgan's *Wanamurraganya* (1989), Ruby Langford Ginibi's *Real Deadly* (1992) and *My Bundjalung People*

(1994c), Rita and Jackie Huggins's *Auntie Rita* (1994), Rosemary van den Berg's *No Options. No Choice!* (1994) and Doris Pilkington's *Follow the Rabbit-Proof Fence* (1995). In other words, such narratives are no longer mainly autobiographical but biographical. This chapter focuses largely on the autobiographical phase.

The burgeoning of women's narratives may be related to a change in the structure of Aboriginal society. An examination of this change makes it possible for us to understand what Jane M. Jacobs (quoting Connell) calls the 'historicity of gender', that is, the way gender relations have been transformed through colonisation (Jacobs, 1989:92). In recent generations women have started to occupy a more prominent role in communal as well as in family life, which has become, in Marcia Langton's term, 'matrifocal' (Langton, 1981:18). This fact has been commented on by many Aboriginal women, including Sally Morgan:

> In a lot of Aboriginal families, actually, the women are very strong. In many families I know they carry the weight of the family . . . In most Aboriginal families there is always at least one strong female character with a grandma or an auntie or somebody like that who holds everything together. (Morgan quoted in Bird and Haskell, 1992:7, 19)

A number of reasons have been put forward to explain why Aboriginal women are more often heads of households. These include the itinerant nature of Aboriginal men's employment; the high rate of imprisonment of Aboriginal men; the greater incidence of alcoholism among Aboriginal men (Burgmann, 1984:30); and the fact that under the Australian welfare system it has been more beneficial for an unemployed father to live separated from the family unit (ibid.; Pettman, 1992b:30). According to Roberta Sykes,

> one in four black males will be dead by the age thirty [sic], and two of the remaining three will be incarcerated or caught up in the justice system. This means that . . . at least three out of every four black women will sleep alone, will bring up children without the benefit of black paternal presence, and will have no black male with whom to share their lives. (Sykes, 1984:67)

In this cultural climate Aboriginal women have become leaders not only in the family but also in the community generally as Shirley Smith (also known as Colleen Perry) describes:

> In the black world, years ago, it was a man's world. When I was running around here, thirty years ago, there wasn't too many black women going to jails and talking to every Tom, Dick and Harry or running to court or going looking in pubs for different people and drinking. They was all home. Because it was a man's world. But now, the men have got no responsibility. They've shifted everything on to the woman. Now when a man comes home, his wife is out working. Some of them get better money than the men. Black women are running things, saying things. Was a time when they'd be home having babies and saying nothing. (Smith, 1977:249)

In her discussion of the community roles of Aboriginal women Patricia Grimshaw refers to Diane Barwick's report that in Victoria in the decades after 1860 women were more prepared than men to take up political action in relation to white management of Aboriginal reserves (Grimshaw, 1980:699). Grimshaw also quotes Vera Lovelock's comments on the prominence of women activists up to the 1970s (ibid.:693). Patsy Cohen, whose autobiographical narrative traces the 'five black matriarchs' of her Aboriginal community, comments on the psychological reasons why women have become family and community leaders:

> I think after the contact with white people came in and destroyed the cultural kinship system and the way that blackfellers lived, they upset everything. They stripped the men of all their pride and respect and I think it was these, the likes of these old matriarchs, that sort of kept the men goin'. They were really strong for the men, these old women, 'cause just imagine in them times the hardship and the pressure that's put on them. (Cohen and Somerville, 1990:109)

Whereas anthropological research focused in the past on men, more recently there has been extensive debate about the place of women in pre-contact society. Patricia O'Shane (1976:32) and Eve

Fesl (1984:111) have argued that in a hunter–gatherer society Aboriginal women had a great degree of independence. Annette Hamilton follows a similar line of argument, but suggests that, despite women's economic independence, men specialised in religious and philosophical power—considered intrinsically more important—and women were subject to control and manipulation by men as objects of value (A. Hamilton, 1975:170). Diane Bell has asserted that women had substantial independence in both ritual and economic terms and a separate gender-specific power base (see Pettman, 1992b:25). Francesca Merlan discusses the dichotomous nature of gender relations but insists that they were not colonising (Merlan, 1988:54).

Although the matrifocal nature of contemporary Aboriginal society has been commented upon extensively, Jan Pettman warns us not to romanticise Aboriginal women as matriarchs. This is because to do so may conceal the pressure on Aboriginal families, and overestimate the ability of Aboriginal women to protect and sustain themselves and their families (Pettman, 1992b:30). We need to remember that the 'black matriarchy' is a product of the poverty-induced conditions of a racially oppressed proletarian subgroup. 'The strength of women in the "hearth group" of traditional society', Burgmann (quoting Schultz) observes, 'may have lingered on into urban society in that women are the ones who often "hold the community together", but it is external factors that have forced women into leadership positions' (Burgmann, 1984:29).

As heads of households, Aboriginal women have assumed responsibility for the continuation and transmission of Aboriginal values and practices, and act as a counter to outside influences, as O'Shane (1976:33) and Daylight and Johnstone (1986:2) have pointed out. The same is true of black women in the USA (Reagon, 1982: 81–2; hooks, 1990b:42). Aboriginal women's autobiographies foreground gender-specific strategies of resistance to white racism, such as the maintenance of the family and a distinct way of life. This has been in opposition to the government policy (initiated by the state-instituted 'Aborigines' and 'Aborigines Protection' Acts of the late nineteenth and early twentieth centuries) of removing children with 'white' blood from their families and allocating them either to city dwellers as domestics or to white farmers as domestics and station-workers, positions where they were often used virtually as slave labour. Roberta Sykes has described the forced removal of these children from their families as 'a major crime against Aboriginal people and humanity generally, and . . . arguably the most despicable white activity of the past century' (Sykes, 1991:181).

Alice Nannup, a Yindjibarndi woman, was born in 1911. In *When the Pelican Laughed* (1992), which spans the period 1905–92, she describes being taken away from her family and working as an underpaid and non-paid domestic from the age of twelve. Of the Western Australian Government's 1905 Aborigines' Act—which brought about the removal of children from their parents—she says: 'they wanted to disconnect people from their past [and] they meant for us to never find our way back home' (Nannup, 1992:70, 120). Her story culminates when she finally finds her 'way back home' at the age of fifty-four. 'They might have taken me away from my home', she says, 'but they didn't take my home away from me' (ibid.:204). Coercive attempts at resocialising and individualising Aboriginal people encounter strong resistance in the affirmation of home, Nannup's family—specifically her mother—and the Aboriginal way of life (both with her mother and in the raising of her own children). She talks with pride about her mother's and her own bush cooking (traditional and white). The disgusting food that Aboriginal people were forced to eat on the Moore River mission was a tactic, she says, 'to deliberately lower us; well, degrade us really' (ibid.:64). She asserts with pride: 'I wasn't brought up like that. My mother was a beautiful cook and we ate lovely meals back home' (ibid.). She also talks about the effectiveness of traditional health cures, and the power of spirituality. Nannup's mother is her link with Aboriginal spirituality: she assigns the young Alice her totem. Through this narrative Nannup affirms the power of the spiritual world and its intervention in her life at times of crisis. She concludes her narrative with an affirmation of Aboriginal law when she visits a pool in her family country and appeases the old snake spirit: 'That's beautiful isn't it?' she says, 'To keep your tradition and never let it go' (ibid.:224).

Another example of Nannup's attachment to her family's way of life and her resistance to white culture is her use of Aboriginal language. She relates how first her white father and then officials at the Moore River mission forbad her to use 'language'. In opposition to these directives the children found a form of resistance in their native tongue, and a means of cursing the people who had taken them away from their parents: 'we used to curse those Campbells. We used to say to each other in language that they were terrible for taking us away from our home, and we wished something would happen to them. Oh, we used to be nasty' (ibid.:56).

One effect of separating children from their parents and extended family was to diminish the use of Aboriginal languages. Nannup describes how in this way she lost her fluency in the language. She also describes how, despite broken promises to send her to school, she learnt to write English by copying jam-jar labels: she's very proud of this subversive tactic, and relates the story several times. Being able to write enables her to keep in touch with friends—a privilege denied her as a child, when her white 'employers' refused to reply to letters from her family at a time when she herself was unable to read or write.

The use of 'lingo' in Langford's *Don't Take Your Love to Town* (1988) similarly implies solidarity and resistance. It affirms a sense of intimacy and common experience in the shared gaol-cell, for example, where Nobby and James talk about women and sex. In addition, throughout the book, Langford makes abundant use of 'lingo' to describe the police, whose relationship with Aboriginal people has always been extensive and often brutal. The use of 'lingo' for spiritual purposes further marks off Aboriginal experience. One such example is Ruby's incantation, given to her by her mother to ward off the spirit of her dead son. It is significant that, on this occasion, Ruby becomes temporarily deaf after Bill's death, and is able to hear only her mother speak, presumably in 'lingo'.

These strategies of resistance are of paramount importance, given the intensive surveillance of Aboriginal people. Aboriginal people brought up on missions had their mobility restricted; they were also prohibited from mixing with their families, and their time was regimented. When they left the mission to work, the Department of Aborigines exercised control over their money, where they went, and whom they could work for; it could also intervene in their personal lives, and interrogate them at any time. Throughout her narrative Nannup deplores the lack of Aboriginal rights; she repeatedly refers to herself and other Aboriginal people as 'slaves' (1992:52, 143). Although Aboriginal people have introduced the term 'slavery' into their own rewriting of post-invasion history (Fesl, 1993a:340; Huggins and Huggins, 1994:39), the word continues to be generally disavowed in white histories.

## Subjugated knowledges

Strategic resistance can be explored more fully in terms of Foucault's notion of 'the insurrection of subjugated knowledges', which he glosses as 'the immediate emergence of historical contents . . . that have been buried and disguised' (Foucault, 1980:81). What comes to light in this process are knowledges that have been 'disqualified as inadequate to their task or insufficiently elaborated: [they are] naive knowledges, located low down on the hierarchy, beneath the required level of cognition or scientificity' (ibid.:82).

From these disinterred practices we can reconstruct what Foucault describes as a 'genealogy' of knowledge. This makes it possible to establish a historical knowledge of struggles and the 'use of [such] knowledge tactically today' (ibid.:83). But these genealogies can arise only when 'the tyranny of globalising discourses with their hierarchy and all their privileges . . . [is] eliminated' (ibid.). The discourses that have tyrannised Aboriginal people are those which articulate government policies. These policies were initiated with the formation of the Aborigines Protection Board and the passing of Acts that are foregrounded in the autobiographical narratives I am discussing, namely the Aborigines Act, the Western Australian version of which was repealed only in 1963.

In tracing the decolonising counter-discourse of contemporary Aboriginal culture, I take my cue from Foucault, who warns against the reinscription of a totalising discourse:

it will be no part of our concern to provide a solid and homogeneous theoretical terrain for all these dispersed genealogies, nor to descend upon them from on high with some kind of halo of theory that would unite them. Our task, on the contrary, will be to expose and specify the issue at stake in this opposition, this struggle, this insurrection of knowledges against the institutions and against effects of the knowledge and power that invests scientific discourse. (ibid.:87)

Nevertheless, Foucault warns of the need to be constantly vigilant: 'is it not perhaps the case that these fragments of genealogies are no sooner brought to light, that the particular elements of the knowledge that one seeks to disinter are no sooner accredited and put into circulation, than they run the risk of re-codification, re-colonisation?' (ibid.:86). To trace the genealogy of subjugated knowledges embedded in Aboriginal women's autobiography is to highlight two aspects of the genre: the significance of the family, and the performative aspect of story-telling. I will begin by exploring further the issue of the family.

I have argued that it is important to understand the Aboriginal family in its historical context and the role it plays in resisting white culture. This role is gendered. As keepers of the family, Aboriginal women are the bearers of 'naive knowledges', counter-discourses to white culture. Aboriginal women's autobiography reconstructs the 'historical contents' of subjugated knowledges, and those 'historical contents' are gendered. Their stories describe the family as a strategy of resistance; 'domesticity', in bell hooks's words, is 'a site of subversion' (hooks, 1990b:48). A genealogy of the family is thus crucially important in view of the devastating effects of the Aborigines Act.

The importance of family in Aboriginal women's lives and narratives goes against the grain of that First World feminism which sees the family as a means of oppression. However, as black feminists in both the UK and USA have pointed out, the family has a different significance for minority constituencies. According to Hazel Carby, for example, in the UK 'the black family has been a site of political and cultural resistance to racism' (Carby, 1982:214); Valerie Amos and Pratibha Parmar similarly reclaim the notion of family from white feminists and anthropologists in order to 'locate the Black family more firmly in the historical experiences of Black people' (Amos and Parmar, 1984:11); and Bev Fisher argues that the family, as 'the last barricade between minority and lower-class people and the oppression of the state', is 'a shelter [from] the abuses of a classist, racist, sexist society' (Fisher, 1977:13). The same is true of other minority groups; Keya Ganguly suggests that in her immigrant community, 'the family remains the only "traditional" cultural support and source of renewal for the women' (Ganguly, 1992:45).

In their representation of family life, Aboriginal women's autobiographies such as Nannup's are laced with descriptions of the practice of home-making, and with talk about traditional foods and cooking, health remedies and wisdom. The naming of all these things is an important act of decolonisation, a reinscribing of domestic and geographical space. The construction of a genealogy of the family is also a process of articulating what Foucault calls 'naive knowledges' which are 'located low down on the hierarchy, beneath the required level of cognition or scientificity' (Foucault, 1980:82). And indeed at least one white male critic has found the constant references to cooking in Aboriginal women's autobiography a mark of trivialisation, as Robyn McCarron (1991:19) has noted.

In these autobiographical narratives, the 'naive knowledges' of Aboriginal women exist side by side with the scientific knowledge they have acquired from white culture. Ellie Gaffney's *Somebody Now* (1989), for instance, is in large part a history of her nursing career, studded with references to western notions of health, medicine and hygiene. But it is interspersed also with stories from an incommensurate discourse, namely traditional lore and local wisdom. Here is an example:

Husbands of pregnant women are forbidden to hunt and kill during their wives' pregnancies.
   This tale I am about to tell is a true story I experienced with two Torres Strait Island women in my nursing career. It could have been a coincidence, but it is strange. The women's husbands had decided to go deer hunting during this period against the elders' wishes. Whilst hunting, they shot a deer each. One of the deer was still showing signs of life so the older of the hunters butted the deer's mouth and then shot it through the heart. His wife gave birth to a baby boy with a hare lip and a cleft palate, and a hole in his heart. That child died at the age of two-and-a-half. The other hunter merely scalped his deer for the six pointer

horn. His wife gave birth to a beautiful girl, except she was an anancephalic [sic]. An anancephalic [sic] is a child born usually fully formed, except it has no scalp bone and the brain is exposed; the child usually dies in a few hours. In this case, it died soon after birth. In my twenty-six years of nursing, that was the second anancephalic [sic] I had witnessed. They are a rarity. (Gaffney, 1989:33)

Story-telling and the narration of life histories have an important role within the family. Late in her life, at the age of seventy-eight, Alice Nannup is able to consolidate her resistance to white colonisation in the counter-discourse of her own narrative. That this action is politically important to her she asserts several times. The telling of the past is necessary for several reasons. She sees the book as an important documentation of the past both for her family's sake and for the rewriting of history. Of the latter she wryly remarks: 'You won't find anything about the hell we went through in history books, but it happened, every little bit of it is true' (Nannup, 1992:218). Her stories, she explains, are already circulating within her family, and among her motives in putting the book together is to consolidate their history: 'I think it's important to get all my stories down into the one book. That way my family, and their family, and their family, and so on, will always have them' (ibid.:217). She also wants to make her story public knowledge, and thus acquaint others with the history of Aboriginal people under colonisation: '[I] hope that all people, young, old, black, white, will read this book and see how life was for people in my time' (ibid.:218).

I would like to look more closely now at the context in which this counter-discourse of Nannup and other Aboriginal women emerges. This is to raise again the issue of the positioning of Aboriginal literature within white discourse. Both Larbalestier and Muecke have focused on how Aboriginal writing is constrained by the white discourses that mobilise it. Without denying that Aboriginal literature is inevitably mediated by white discourse, I want to emphasise the fact that Aboriginal writers and story-tellers do indeed have agency in its production and circulation, and that the enunciative act itself, that is, the act of articulating their texts, implies an Aboriginal readership or audience. I will now examine more closely the enunciative act and its social framing.

## Story-telling

Orality is an important aspect of Aboriginal culture. Stories and songs played a crucial role in traditional Aboriginal cultures, as Catherine H. Berndt has pointed out:

> because Aborigines were traditionally non-literate, fundamental instructions and information about [the land and its resources] came through words, in word-of-mouth transmission—not so much through drawings, cave paintings and visual symbols, but predominantly through *words*, spoken and sung: stories and songs were a major means of transmitting and sustaining Aboriginal culture. (Berndt, 1985:93)

Paul Carter talks about the 'spatial history' of Aboriginal culture in terms of story-telling and song. He begins with a quotation from an anthropologist: '"the women sang the songs of the country as they travelled through it" . . . Travelling and story-telling are inseparable from each other. The country is not the setting of the stories, but the stories and songs themselves' (Carter, 1987:346).

Contemporary Aboriginal culture is also characterised by orality. Margaret Somerville relates that, while working with Patsy Cohen on her life history, many of the Aboriginal people they interviewed attested to the importance of orality by 'insisting that Aboriginal culture was what their elders told them' (Somerville, 1990:31). Jackie Huggins also asserts that 'the dominant discourse for Aboriginal people is through our oral traditions' (Huggins and Tarrago, 1990:140), and that the oral transmission of history and culture 'was one of the many forms of resistance strategies that Aboriginals employed against the colonising forces' (Huggins, 1991a:89). It is important to be as aware of the oral nature of Aboriginal women's narratives as of the gender-specificity of the family histories they record because, as Susan Geiger reminds us, 'for most of the world's women, literacy is a very recent possibility, and of the one-quarter of the total population that remains illiterate, nearly 70 percent is female' (Geiger, 1986:335). While the dialogic process of interviewing and collaboration has been formally foregrounded in some recent transcriptions of Aboriginal story-telling (e.g. Muecke, 1983), texts packaged as autobiographical narratives generally have the format of the interview process (apparently) erased. I would suggest, however, that traces of the oral genesis of the text remain. The oral or 'telling' aspect of autobiographies can be uncovered by focusing on the relationship between the narrator and, in the first instance, the listener. The dynamics of the act of telling reveals something about the social and cultural positioning of the narrative.

*When the Pelican Laughed* is the edited transcription of interviews with Nannup by two younger people, one of whom is of Aboriginal descent and the grandson of a long-time friend of hers. This autobiography is essentially an oral text, or at least one that was conceived orally. The oral inscription of Nannup's narrative is quite striking. We notice (as readers) that the narrator often addresses the reader or listener directly, as for example in the last sentence of the narrative: 'you see, forty-two years later I got back to my family, and sixty-four years from when I left Point Samson, I got back to make my peace with my country' (Nannup, 1992:224). The direct address ('you see') occurs elsewhere in the book; it points to the act of telling, and invokes the reader or listener repeatedly. The original listeners, as I mentioned, were people well known to Nannup. Many recent autobiographies by Aboriginal women that are derived from transcripts of oral narratives are narrated to either a member of the 'author's' family (as in the case of Daisy and Gladys Corunna in *My Place* and Rita and Jackie Huggins in *Auntie Rita*), or another Aborigine (as in *Mum Shirl*), or else a close white friend (as in *Ingelba*). The frequent use of the vocative form of address evokes a sense of intimacy and trust, as well as the immediacy of the listener, whose presence is as palpable as in speech or conversation. The anonymous white reader 'overhears', as it were, this 'conversation' between an Aboriginal narrator and her family and friends. Sometimes this places the reader in the position of a voyeur as when Nan tells Sally of her most personal pain and bitterness in *My Place* (Morgan, 1987:337, 351–2). But always our attention is drawn to the specifically social nature of the language acts which constitute the original oral narrative. These invoke the communal bond between teller and listener, and reinforce an awareness of language as social interaction.

The oral narratives I am talking about epitomise Walter Benjamin's thesis that story-telling is an essentially social act which rests upon 'the ability to exchange experiences' and to offer counsel to the listener (Benjamin, 1973:83, 86). Companionship is an important aspect of story-telling. The sense of exchanging experiences rather than simply information—and therefore of giving counsel—is evident in Nannup's narrative. It is manifest in the 'moral' of her many tales of self-assertion, and in the advice she gives her children (and, by extension, other Aboriginal people) on dealing with racism: 'I taught my kids to stand up for themselves, and not let other people treat them like dirt on account of being Aboriginal' (Nannup, 1992:191).

Benjamin's suggestion that story-telling is drawn from 'the realm of living speech' (Benjamin, 1973:87) is also exemplified in Nannup's narrative. Story-telling is for Benjamin the 'art of repeating stories' and is made up of 'layers of a variety of retellings' (ibid.:91, 93). I have drawn attention already to the fact that Nannup sees her stories as narratives that will continue to be retold and reread in her family. Her own book, for example, opens with the narrator repeating stories her mother had told her. Janine Little has similarly observed that the mother–daughter exchange in the collaborative (auto)biography *Auntie Rita* symbolises the wider experience of Murri story-telling (Little, 1994:52).

Reviewers and critics of these texts often mistakenly refer to them as having been 'written' by the Aboriginal narrator. It is, of course, a fact that several Aboriginal women have written their autobiographies, albeit with non-Aboriginal editorial intervention: examples include Sally Morgan, Glenyse Ward, Labumore (Elsie Roughsey), Mabel Edmund, Ellie Gaffney and Doris Pilkington. But the majority have been transcribed either wholly or in part from oral narratives—including those of Eliza Kennedy, Shirley Smith, Della Walker, Patsy Cohen and Alice Nannup. Even Sally Morgan's *My Place* is partly a transcription of taped conversations with her family (Morgan, 1988). It is not surprising, therefore, that such narratives frequently invoke the presence of a listener or reader. As performative acts—drawing upon a repertoire to meet the social requirements and conditions of the occasion—these texts are above all contingent and local.

Walter J. Ong discusses the 'relatedness' of oral texts, their 'here and now communal expectations' and how an oral milieu affects the composition of a text and its interpretation (Ong, 1986:150, 155, 164). Traces of these aspects of the social enunciation and performance of their stories are evident in Aboriginal women's narratives. To ignore the social and material conditions of these performative utterances is to fall into the trap that Foucault describes. It is to decontextualise and dehistoricise the text, to aestheticise it in the name of the institutional discourse of literary criticism. Thus the text is recolonised. Only by treating the text as contingent and local can we avoid reducing it to a merely textual phenomenon, and therefore avoid subsuming it into a depoliticised and universalising discourse.

## Recollection

I am not suggesting that the oral basis of Nannup's narrative is completely 'pure' or unadulterated. White editors and publishers mediate such texts, and Aboriginal narratives are to some extent determined by the white discourses that constitute them. To suggest, however, as Muecke does (by way of Foucault's repressive hypothesis) that the recent proliferation of Aboriginal writing has less to do with the agency of Aboriginal people than with the material conditions that produce such literature for a white population now 'ready' to consume it, shifts our focus away from contemporary Aboriginal knowledge and Aboriginality. Muecke's argument passes over the social and gendered nature of texts whose oral nature evokes the social act of retelling experience. But, to concede that a white readership views these texts through the lens of its own culturally-specific history, I would like to offer one suggestion as to why these books have been popular with white readers.

A striking feature of Nannup's narrative is the repetition of phrases such as 'looking back', 'when I think back', 'if I only knew then what I know today' and 'I realise how much I was denied' (Nannup, 1992:71, 120, 211). These phrases differentiate Nannup's speaking position (the present) from the events (the past) about which she speaks. The narrative mode is recollection: a (re)reading of the narrator's own life, it is often punctuated with a sense of amazement and disbelief at the injustices she and other Aboriginal people endured. She re-evaluates the past from the perspective of a present marked by changed and changing conditions for Aboriginal people. Formerly powerless as a child, adolescent and struggling mother, she speaks now as the progenitor of a hundred children, grand-children and great-grandchildren, as a prodigal daughter reunited with her family, and as a published author.

Because most Aboriginal women's autobiographies are narrated by grandmothers, they focus necessarily on the past. I suggest that the injustices they portray are seen by most white readers as belonging to a period of history before our own time. As a result, the shock experienced by many white readers is cushioned by relief that 'things are not like that now'. A sense of outrage at past iniquities does not necessarily open the eyes of a white community to the continuing prevalence of racism, and to the dispossession and injustices that Aboriginal people suffer today. This is not to discount what I see as the 'educative' value of these autobiographies for many white readers. As Ruby Langford Ginibi suggests, life stories such as her own are 'probably the only information that a lot of students get that puts the Aboriginal point of view' (Langford, 1991:129); many other Aboriginal women writers and story-tellers emphasise their professional educative role (e.g. Torres, 1993:103). The proliferation of Aboriginal autobiographies has had a discernible effect on white cultural amnesia.

However, these stories are not narrated only to a white audience. It is important to take into account the oral nature of these narratives and the fact that the originary enunciative act of oral story-telling from which these written texts evolve is framed by both Aboriginal and white listeners. Such stories provide an 'education' for a contemporary generation of Aboriginal people who have not lived through the times these grandmothers speak about, and who in some cases did not even know they were of Aboriginal blood until late in their childhood (Morgan, 1987; Cohen quoted in Somerville, 1990:34). Many Aboriginal writers aim their texts quite consciously at a white market. Roberta Sykes comments that although black writing 'is very important, it's equally important that whites read it' (Sykes, 1988:83); Jackie Huggins and Isabel Tarrago point out that Aboriginal authors must take a white audience into account in order to sell books (Huggins and Tarrago, 1990:143–4). None the less, it is important to keep in mind that despite this conscious marketing strategy, Aboriginal texts (as exemplified by women's autobiographical narratives) are hybrid in their enunciation, since they are directed at both Aboriginal and white readers.

Now that Aboriginal women have come to occupy a focal position in the family, their leadership is manifest also in the general community, where women are prominent. Statistically they are better educated than Aboriginal men (Burgmann, 1984:20); they are employed in greater numbers (Daylight and Johnstone, 1986:135) and at a marginally higher status (Burgmann, 1984:32). Many Aboriginal women autobiographers who were born in the 1930s became political leaders during the 1960s. Edmund and Gaffney in particular had high-profile political careers. Edmund was a shire councillor, a federal commissioner and an endorsed ALP candidate; in 1986 she was awarded an Order of Australia. Gaffney is also well known in Aboriginal affairs, mainly in the fields of nursing and education, but also in Aboriginal media organisations in Queensland. Smith and Tucker were awarded MBEs, and Simon (who was born in 1902) is hailed as 'probably the first Aboriginal woman to be made a J.P.' (Simon, 1978:14). Many of these women have a high community profile and some—like Langford Ginibi—appear regularly in the media. Several (Pilkington, Cohen and Crawford) obtained a tertiary education after they had raised their families. Clearly they write and speak from a position of social prestige and achievement, and their work is a conscious articulation of an oppressed history. In narratives of recollection, each (re)reads her own life, re-evaluating the past from the changed conditions of the present. Their personal success highlights the huge gulf in between.

## Oral story to written text: Evelyn Crawford

The story-tellers of Aboriginal autobiographical narratives, I have suggested, address both a black and a white audience. In the case of narratives recorded orally, however, the most immediate addressee is the interviewer, who records, transcribes and subsequently edits the manuscript. This enunciative positioning is often rendered invisible in discussions of Aboriginal women's autobiographical narratives. Yet the manner in which these processes 'frame' the texts is crucial to the way in which memory and narrative are constructed and read.

As a genre, Aboriginal autobiographical narratives in general have mapped the transition in contemporary Aboriginal culture from an oral to a literate society. A substantial proportion of Aboriginal women's autobiographical narratives and life stories have been narrated orally by an Aboriginal 'author' who may in fact be literate; they have then been recorded, transcribed and edited by either an Aboriginal or non-Aboriginal 'interviewer'. A smaller proportion of narratives have been written directly on to the page. Sometimes a collaborative writing process is acknowledged (as, for example, in early print-runs of Langford's *Don't Take Your Love to Town* where copyright is shared); in other instances editors are not credited with a collaborative role (as in autobiographical narratives by Sally Morgan, Glenyse Ward, Marnie Kennedy, Mabel Edmund and Ellie Gaffney). With reference to Evelyn Crawford's *Over My Tracks* (1993), I would like to examine in more detail the technology of the relationship (in stories that have been narrated orally) between the Aboriginal story-teller and her audiences. These include both her interviewer/editor and her wider readership at a time when Aboriginal women's knowledge is in transition from an oral to a written form.

In Crawford's narrative that transition is paralleled by the narrator's increased mobility in the white community. This occurs around the time of her husband Gong's death in 1974, when Crawford becomes involved in the schooling of her youngest child, and eventually rises in the education system to work variously as an Aboriginal Teacher's Aide, a Home-School Co-ordinator and a TAFE Aboriginal Regional Co-ordinator. Before her husband died Crawford had lived largely in black communities.

The black American writer bell hooks also writes about the transition in her own life from a black to a white community. She describes how the writing of autobiography was a way to 'remember and hold to the legacy' of growing up in a southern black community, an experience subsequently lost as a result of her living in predominantly white communities:

> Black southern folk experience was the foundation of the life around me when I was a child; that experience no longer exists in many places where it was once all of life that we knew. Capitalism, upward mobility, assimilation of other values have all led to rapid disintegration of black folk experience or in some cases the gradual wearing away of that experience. (hooks, 1991:1038)

Crawford describes a similar process of assimilation in Australian society. She describes being a member of a senior citizens' group in Broken Hill, and how quite some time passed before her white friends even knew she was Aboriginal (Crawford, 1993:286). Her attitude towards this transition from a black to a white community is ambivalent. Her work in schools and TAFE colleges makes her an advocate of white education for Aboriginal children and adolescents. But she sees this as a strategic necessity; in other ways she resists assimilation. bell hooks recalls that when she went to university her mother said to her, 'you can take what the white people have to offer but you do not have to love them' (hooks, 1990a:342). Similarly, Crawford maintains a distance from her white colleagues in schools: 'I didn't let myself really *like* any of the people I worked with. I respected them. They were my colleagues. But I never let it get to the "they're my friend" stage. What would we have in common?' (Crawford, 1993:280, original emphasis). Distance is here a strategic resistance to assimilation into white culture.

Crawford's sense of her separateness from white 'settler' culture is illustrated in another of her anecdotes. It describes the high point of her upward mobility in white culture, namely her invitation to the Queen's opening of the Darling Harbour Project in 1988. She describes this occasion as 'a big reward' for all the hard times in the past, and something that gives her a 'new lease on life' (ibid.:312). On this occasion Crawford ironically stages herself as not a colonised but an indigenous subject who, in treading the red carpet before the Queen arrives, reclaims her right to walk where she chooses in her own country (ibid.:308). This incident humorously demonstrates her claim to a distinct and indigenous identity and sovereignty.

We can read the last four chapters of *Over My Tracks* as documenting Crawford's transition into the white community and the literate world where she is first a student and then a teacher, and the first three as recalling her traditional Aboriginal learning and her relationship with her Aboriginal teachers. They contain detailed descriptions of traditional practices in which Crawford was instructed: setting up camp, bush cooking, bush medicine, tracking, collecting bush tucker, reading the weather, clan-group relationships, childbirth, finding water, and painting. All of these knowledges, which have been subjugated in white society, are contrasted with the educational methodology of white classrooms.

It becomes clear from these carefully detailed descriptions that Crawford's narrative, like Nannup's, is educative and archival in function and that the knowledges it documents are gendered. Some commentators play down the importance of tradition in contemporary Aboriginal literature (Ariss, 1988:136); but in many Aboriginal women's autobiographical narratives the narrators see themselves as custodians of knowledges that must be recorded and passed on. Although the main recipients of such knowledge would appear to be young people in the extended family and the wider Aboriginal community, the education of white people is also on the agenda. Aboriginal women who produce autobiographical narratives, however, insist that they address the black community, and most immediately their own families. Marnie Kennedy, for example, writes: '[My] story is for my grandchildren and for [all] Aboriginal children. They cannot know the history of our people before the white man came but they should know this part of their history' (Kennedy, 1985:1).

The education of children is an important issue for Aboriginal women, as young people make up a large percentage of the Aboriginal population; according to the 1991 Census, 61 per cent of Aboriginal people in Western Australia are under twenty-five. The activist Barbara Flick comments:

It has only been recently that the Murri women's contribution to the maintenance of our culture and existence in the face of the destruction of our communities has been recorded . . . We struggle for the rights of our children to their own culture. They have the right to learn about our religion and our struggle and they need to be instructed by us in the ways in which this world makes sense to us. (Flick, 1990:65)

'Our history as Murri women', she adds, 'lives and thrives in our own oral history tradition' (ibid.). Ketu Katrak—quoting Buchi Emecheta—makes a similar point about the role of women in Nigerian society: 'women are born story-tellers. We keep the history . . . we conserve things and we never forget. What I do is not clever or unusual. It is what my aunt and my grandmother did, and their mothers before them' (Katrak, 1989:174). Because changing factors in contemporary Aboriginal culture have obliged women increasingly to take on the role of parenting in Aboriginal families, they therefore play an important part in the maintenance of contemporary culture by passing on information that traditionally has been transmitted orally. Jacques Le Goff (quoting Georges Balandier) describes how in preliterate societies there are memory specialists, custodians of knowledge who are 'the memory of the society' (Le Goff, 1992:56). To some extent Aboriginal women play this role in contemporary culture. The memory they preserve is, I have argued, gendered; we may well be observing in contemporary Aboriginal society what Le Goff terms 'the feminine function of the conservation of remembrance' (ibid.:90).

The recording of this information in print and its publication as autobiographical narratives therefore mark the transition from an oral to a literate culture. It has been suggested that neither traditional oral narrative nor contemporary autobiography foregrounds factual information. Walter Ong, for example, states that 'in functionally oral cultures the past is not felt as an itemised terrain, peppered with verifiable and disputed "facts" or bits of information' (Ong, 1982:98). This is a point that John Murphy also emphasises: 'oral recollection inclines towards the figurative rather than the specific, to tropes rather than to facts' (Murphy, 1986:164). bell hooks, commenting on her own autobiographical writing, says: 'I felt that I was not as concerned with accuracy of detail as I was with evoking in writing the state of mind, the spirit of a particular moment' (hooks, 1991:1038).

The brief list of traditional knowledges which Crawford itemises in precise detail indicates, however, that her narrative is quite different from the oral narratives Ong and Murphy describe. Because Aboriginal women are committed to passing on traditional culture, facts and information form a large part of their autobiographical narratives. Mudrooroo, for example, remarks that Labumore's autobiographical narrative *An Aboriginal Mother Tells of the Old and the New* (1984) is 'a veritable encyclopaedia of Aboriginal beliefs and practices' (Narogin, 1990:161). Hence the collaboration of Aboriginal women with white interviewers and editors, and with mainstream white presses. Disinclined to take on the task of writing a whole book themselves, and yet compelled to translate traditional knowledge from an oral into a literate form in order to preserve it for future generations, Aboriginal oral historians and story-tellers choose to collaborate with white scribes. In the transition from orality to literature, story becomes history, at least in the sense that Aboriginal historians construct it; namely, a discourse that establishes continuities between past and present.

Despite this shift into literate modes of thought and reading, Aboriginal women's autobiographical narratives retain much of their oral origins. Ong makes the point that in oral cultures story-tellers and singers borrow, adapt, repeat and share old and familiar themes and stories. This is certainly true of these Aboriginal narratives, which frequently quote family elders. Crawford's narrative, for example, opens with a reference both to her children and her father. 'I tell my kids, "I remember this happenin'"', she says, and a little later quotes one of her father's maxims: 'My Dad used to say, "Your friends are where you find them"' (Crawford, 1993:ix). The reported speech and mention of her children imply a network of oral narrative stretching across several generations. It precedes and underlies the staged narration, recording and transcription of Evelyn Crawford's life stories—that is, their transition into print. The oral story-teller's role is both preserved and transformed. This cross-generational network of oral narrative demonstrates that the social role of story-telling survives in Aboriginal women's autobiographical narratives despite their transition into the privatised world of literature.

In these translations—from oral to literate culture, from black to white community, and from the private to the public sphere—the story-teller's narrative is transformed and reconstructed according to the mode of production. (One small but significant example of such mutations is the fact that while Crawford makes a point of explaining that the Aboriginal pronunciation of Mootwingee is Mootawingee—and uses this spelling throughout the narrative— the map opposite page one reproduces the white rather than the Aboriginal spelling.) We must be aware of the speaking position of the Aboriginal narrator, and examine how it is framed in the production of the text. Nor should we forget that the print narrative transcribed from Aboriginal oral histories and stories is the product of a collaborative and intersubjective process in which white technologies transform the oral text.

Because the comments that frame Crawford's narrative construct it as a 'personal' narrative which emerges out of 'friendship', the text is read accordingly as a statement of friendship. The interviewer and transcriber, Chris Walsh, states in her preface that her relationship with Crawford is that of 'a great friend', and that she and Crawford have 'shared' childhoods and experiences. Her reaction to Crawford's narrative is primarily emotional; she 'laughed until [she] cried, and cried until it hurt'. This implies that readers should identify with Walsh's response—a position reinforced on the back cover: 'Reading her story is like sitting down for a yarn with an old friend'. This intimate positioning of story-teller and interviewer effaces the professional nature of Crawford's relationship with her transcriber. The intimate alignment of white reader with black narrator denies the difference of Aboriginal culture, and ignores Crawford's political role as educator, story-teller and historian; as black American Bernice Reagon has said, 'you don't go into coalition because you just *like* it' (quoted in Kaplan, 1992:132, original emphasis).

It is obvious why Aboriginal women's autobiographical narratives have been such a success with mainstream presses: it is easy to read them as unmediated expressions of experience. Yet it is precisely because most of these women speak from a position of status, power and mobility in white society that they are able to enter the public sphere. Their personal success stories give the white community reason to believe that it is redressing the injustices of the past. As 'representative' figures they create the illusion that mobility within the system is possible for all Aboriginal people. White Australians are thus vindicated. Moreover, because white readers are positioned as 'friends' of the narrator, they don't identify with the white perpetrators of terror, such as the policemen who chain up an old alcoholic Aboriginal man (Crawford, 1993:193). In reading these narratives, white readers develop a better sense of the continuity of Aboriginal history than of white 'settler' culture, which is seen as correspondingly discontinuous with the present. It is difficult for a white reader—'yarning with an old friend', by whom, apparently, we are 'accepted in spite of [our] white skin' (ibid.:viii)—to identify with the white 'settler' Australians of the past. Shielded from identifying with a culture of terror, such readers fail to recognise the continuity with their own history of oppression, and therefore do not realise that 'the time of invasion is the time of now' (D. Rose, 1992:17).

Aboriginal women's autobiographical narratives are necessarily transformed by their entry into the public sphere. That transformation is inscribed both at the enunciative level of the text and in the framing and packaging of the narrative. Mudrooroo, for example, describes the pressures which the publishing apparatus brings to bear on Aboriginal writers and story-tellers to conform to the dictates of genre by producing realist prose. He makes the point that non-Aboriginal editors and publishers, who are inexperienced in any but western genres, need to become sensitive to works which lie outside the European tradition, and specifically to the nuances of Aboriginal English (Mudrooroo, 1994:119). I do not want to suggest that Aboriginal story-tellers are totally passive in the transition from an oral to a literate text (which is, after all, the product of a conscious political decision by Aboriginal women), nor that the oral genesis of their narratives is completely subsumed in the literary production of their books. On the contrary, Aboriginal (hi)stories retain something of their orality in their address to Aboriginal constituencies, and by invoking an oral story-telling network which affirms the continuity of past and present (Brewster, 1994). In recognising the orality of these texts we take into account their sociality, that is, their contractual nature and the political commitment of the Aboriginal women narrators; we acknowledge, in Ross Chambers' words,

> the social fact that narrative mediates human relationships and derives its 'meaning' from them; that, consequently, it depends on social agreements, implicit [or explicit] pacts or contracts, in order to produce exchanges that themselves are a function of desires, purposes, and constraints. (R. Chambers, 1984:4)

## Collaboration and feminism

Since the burgeoning of social anthropology, oral history and the feminist movement in the 1960s, women's autobiographical texts have proliferated. Many result from collaborative projects between advantaged and minority women. Both feminist and minority-discourse theorists argue that the cultural histories such texts invoke are not so much personal and individual as collective. Because feminists read the poetics of autobiography as articulating a patriarchal, mythic and individualistic politics of personal quest, they examine the ways in which women's life stories rewrite this genre. They see the collaborative nature of such texts as definitive of their difference, and argue that on these grounds they should be classified as a genre distinct from autobiography.

Carole Boyce Davies (1992) defines women's collaborative life stories as a 'cross-over genre' which blurs the boundary between orality and writing. Furthermore, by inhabiting a 'conflicted space' where the identities and boundaries of genre are transgressed, they thus destabilise the authorial signature of the written text. The collaboration of editors and interviewers with oral story-tellers is consequently enabling and empowering for minority women, who otherwise would be unable to translate their private stories into that public sphere where they can contest and intervene in the dominant discourse. Davies warns that 'dominant–subordinate relationships' may indeed persist between the editor/interviewer/scribe and the speaker. But such inequities are not further interrogated by Davies, whose unease over the possibility that colonial authority may be reinscribed is subsumed into her general argument that editors and interpreters are 'facilitators' of Aboriginal textual production. As such they are assigned an active and enabling role. The story-tellers are correspondingly passive and (although occasionally threatened with exploitation) mostly enabled.

Caren Kaplan (1992) suggests that women's collaborative life stories constitute an 'out-law genre', which not only destabilises the 'master' genre of autobiography but also reveals the dynamics of power in literary production, distribution and reception. She argues that such life stories deconstruct the middle-class notion of authorial individuality, and that the interactions of the various people involved—editors/interviewers/interpreters/scribes/speakers/story-tellers, and by extension reviewers/theorists/commentators—construct in its place a 'collective authorial entity—a kind of collective consciousness' (Kaplan, 1992:121). These collaborative projects are enabled by 'feminist writing technologies' which open up a space for 'transnational' feminist affiliations and 'transnational coalitions' (ibid.:135). Although Kaplan, like Davies, is sensitive to the imbalance of power between First World and non-metropolitan women (and to the possibility that structures of domination may be re-enacted), she is apparently untroubled by the erasure of difference implied by terms such as 'collective authorial *entity*' and '*collective* consciousness' (my emphasis). These metaphors of the collaborative process are proposed by Kaplan as an alternative to 'essentialist mythologies of identity', which she dismisses without allowing for the fact that some minority constituencies find such mythologies and identities strategically useful and enabling. In its desire to establish acceptable strategies by which feminists can work across cultures, Kaplan's rhetoric is generalising and non-specific to the point of prompting the question—both in the context of her own project and in relation to any claim to transnationality—'why globalise?' (Spivak, 1987:252). A satisfactory answer to this question (in any context) must take account of the contingent social and historical locations of the enquiring subject, the object of her enquiry, and the nature of her intervention. The desire for 'transnational' projects requires a greater scrutiny of the will-to-knowledge than Kaplan demands.

Inevitably, an imbalance of power in projects involving both advantaged and minority women will result in inequities. The point, however, is not to claim some phantasmatic position for feminism—where difference evaporates, and the enquiring subject identifies with the object of her enquiry—but to attend to the specifics of the subjectivities and texts at hand. There will often be a contradiction between the desire for collaboration and ownership of the final product, as Judith Stacey suggests (quoted in Mascia-Lees et al., 1989:21). Nevertheless, radical-feminist issues of sisterhood and the universality of women's oppression (which have been criticised by third-wave feminism) continue to haunt feminism as both 'phantasmatic promise' and 'investment' (I borrow the terms from Butler, 1993:191). These issues can in fact be reread self-reflexively, and mobilised for political resignification. By being (in Jan Pettman's words) 'reconstituted to take account of specificity as well as commonality' (Pettman, 1992a:127), new subject-positions and new interests can be created.

By considering the politics of location in their analyses of collaboration in the production of women's life stories, Davies and Kaplan attempt to empower minority women. In the wake of critiques of First World feminism by minority women, they are anxious to rethink notions such as solidarity and the universality of women's experience (resurrected in the rhetoric of 'transnationality'). Yet by doing so they are in danger, I feel, of erasing the agenda of minority women's political projects. In discussions of texts by minority women, feminism so easily becomes a totalising grand narrative, setting the terms of the debate instead of functioning as a tool with which to analyse the relationship between specific constituencies of different women. If feminism is to be viable in cross-cultural or transnational contexts, it must serve the agendas of minority constituencies, and not use those constituencies to serve the feminism of First World women. Helpful in this respect is Chela Sandoval's call for a new kind of feminism, which she calls 'US Third World feminism', and which would have 'a tactical subjectivity with the capacity to recenter depending upon the kinds of oppression to be confronted' (Sandoval, 1991:14). Feminism can be an enabling project in cross-cultural and transnational contexts, provided we examine why it is invoked.

Alliances with white women have not come readily to Aboriginal women. In many instances class similarities are more dominant than those of gender, and poverty is what links Aboriginal and white people (Langford, 1988:84). Many Aboriginal women have stated that racism concerns them more immediately than sexism (O'Shane, 1976; Huggins, 1987; Sykes, 1984, 1991), and have identified white women as greater oppressors than black men of black women (Fesl, 1984:110). Others have commented that white women are still 'higher on the ladder' than black men ('Ms B' quoted by Burgmann, 1984:38), and are not perceived by black women as oppressed. The invitation to commit themselves to female solidarity with white feminists looks to them like assimilation (Lucashenko, 1994:22). White feminists who want to work on Aboriginal women's texts need to be aware of their own cultural and racial inscription. By investigating their own 'angloality' (Huggins and Saunders, 1993:67), they can come to view their own 'whiteness' as contingent and historically produced (Frankenberg, 1993:233), and in that way help to 'anthropologise the West' (Spivak, 1993:278). It also behoves them to be aware of the agenda of black women. Anthropologists and ethnographers, for example, can accept responsibility for power by 'framing research questions according to the desires of the oppressed group, by choosing to do work that "others" want and need, by being clear for whom they are writing, and by . . . a close and honest scrutiny of the motivations for research' (Mascia-Lees et al., 1989:33). These debates have been rehearsed in the context of Aboriginal culture in Australia not so long ago in the arenas of linguistics, anthropology and history (see, for example, Read, 1990; Cowlishaw, 1992).

The politics of reading minority texts are complex; neither inequities of power nor contradictions of purpose and production can be ignored, but will remain a site of ongoing contestation. A desire to resolve such contradictions and imbalances has produced many unsatisfactory debates about collaborative life stories. In an article theorising the 'collaborative self' in dictated autobiography, Mark A. Sanders criticises 'the essential failure on the part of the critical field to retool', caused by the fact that 'critics have remained doggedly loyal to theories largely unable to address many of the complexities these texts present' (Sanders, 1994:445, 446). He goes on to discuss the discrepancies between written and oral narrative. The rhetorical constructions and literary conventions of writing, he argues, favour thematic linearity, continuity and resolution. An auto-biographical text which is written will thus construct notions of a coherent life story by tracing a trajectory from birth to old age, delineating 'epochs' in the individual's life, and implying a formal progression from one to the other. Invoking Walter J. Ong, he contrasts the technology of writing with the dynamics of oral narratives, which are 'aggregate' rather than 'analytical', 'additive' rather than 'subordinative', and do not 'place concepts and events in relative (and therefore analytic) association, implying a develop-ment or progression of ideas' (ibid.:447).

Sanders borrows from Hayden White's notion that (written) narrative, inasmuch as it reshapes (orally dictated) events and content into familiar generic structures, serves as an 'extended metaphor'. The 'extended metaphor' of the two 'dictated autobiog-raphies' Sanders analyses (*The Autobiography of Malcolm X* and *All God's Dangers*) is that of the quest, which in these texts is informed by 'American myths of the self-made man, the self-reliant individual, and the picaresque trickster' (ibid.:453). In the process of producing a written narrative, Alex Haley (the transcriber) becomes an agent of national mythology, domesticating Malcolm X and familiarising 'a heretofore alien icon in reference to national' (ibid.:454).

Sanders' analysis of the nationalising and mythologising of these texts is accurate in isolating a dominant reading. Once again, however, I have misgivings about the consequences of arguments with structuralist tendencies. Sanders argues that if critics and readers attend to the 'politics of form' they will be able 'to reconstruct the dictator [speaker] as one exerting much more influence over the text' (ibid.:455). This seems at odds with his structuralist analysis of the written narrative. None the less, what he has to say about the appropriative strategies of nationalistic readings of autobiographical narratives can be applied to the reading of Aboriginal women's autobiographical narratives in Australia.

## Nationalism and Aboriginality

Autobiography is one way in which national mythologies are created. In providing a means by which the privatised conscious-ness can be aligned with identities in the public sphere, it enables individuals to come to know themselves as Australians (Sidonie Smith, 1994:9). As a result, individual testimonies can be nationalised: 'the very gesture of proclamation [becomes] one means by which national mythologies conformed individuals to new notions of identity and normative concepts of nationalized subjectivity' (ibid.).

Autobiographical narratives thus come to be identified with specific cultural achievements, and are canonised in various national discourses (such as educational curricula, the media, and tourism) as representative of some aspect of the national mythos. As Mudrooroo has pointed out, Aboriginal autobiographical narratives are popularly read as examples of the 'battler' genre: 'the plotline goes like this. Poor underprivileged person through the force of his or her own character makes it to the top' (Narogin, 1990:149). I would suggest that Aboriginal women autobiographers are often read according to the 'battler' genre, yet it is a myth to assume that Aboriginal people are shaped by the same cultural formations as white Australians, share the same history, and have the same mobility within the public sphere. That myth has assumed renewed importance for white Australians in a post-Mabo period marked by a decisive end to the notion that the state's primary relationship with its indigenous constituency can be defined in terms of the protection and guidance of a people wholly dependent upon its continuing goodwill. The belief that 'we' have survived a troubled past, and will emerge into better times by dint of strength of character and will, is merely a palliative to the guilt and shame that haunt the myth of the nation at its abject borders. But this is why Aboriginal women's autobiographical narratives are often read as personal success stories which, by attesting in turn to the white community's success in redressing past injustices, absolve the consciences of white Australians.

In contemporary Australia we see many examples of Aboriginal culture appropriated by the nationalistic discourses of history, heritage and tourism. Institutional deployments of cultural forms such as Aboriginal autobiographical narratives often result in readings in which the past is individualised, experience is stripped of its collective significance, struggle is depoliticised, and history is constructed in terms of static periods subject to closure. In this process, Aboriginal culture is aestheticised, and Aboriginality is defined culturally rather than politically. An alternative reading would preserve a sense of the oppositional historical consciousness of these texts, and scrutinise the speaking positions of those Aboriginal story-tellers whose subjectivities are ambivalently inscribed in them.

That is why it is important to explore reading strategies that resist subsuming the autobiographical subjects of Aboriginal narratives into myths of individualism and nationalism. The unifying myth of the nation omits other narratives of local struggle, decolonisation, solidarity and community which take place within and in opposition to its borders. Alternative reading strategies therefore consider those features of Aboriginal women's autobiographical narrative that mark its radical difference, such as its oral nature, which has been rendered invisible by the print-oriented discourses of western history and literature (for a discussion of history's exclusion of oral texts see Carter, 1987:326).

The orality of these texts signifies a story-telling network which spans generations and affirms the continuity of Aboriginal culture. Many Aboriginal women's autobiographical texts originate in oral stories that are social and public events. Doris Sommer remarks upon similar aspects in testimonials by Latin American women, which she contrasts with 'the private and even lonely moment of autobiographical writing' (Sommer, 1988:118). The public and interpersonal enunciation of these *testimonios*, she suggests, implies a community quite different from the readership of autobiographies, which are accounts of 'one isolated being speaking for other isolated readers' (ibid.:130). This recalls Walter Benjamin's description of the interaction between novelist and reader: 'A man listening to a story is in the company of the storyteller; even a man reading one shares this companionship. The reader of a novel, however, is isolated, more so than any other reader' (Benjamin, 1973:100). Benjamin thinks of story-telling, on the other hand, as 'the ability to exchange experiences'. According to Sommer, *testimonios* similarly invoke a sense of community: 'when the narrator talks about herself to you, she implies both the existing relationship to other representative selves in the community and potential relationships that extend her community through the text' (Sommer, 1988:118).

The sense that they speak from within a community is as prevalent among Aboriginal women as the precedence taken by that community over other alliances, such as those with white women. As Catrina Felton and Liz Flanagan observe:

> there needs to be a recognition of the importance of Koori women's roles in our communities. Koori women are respected and there are always strong Black women present and speaking out from within our communities. Koori women are active in the struggles which confront our communities daily, but White women don't hear Koori women speak out from within a joint community network. They are only concerned with involving Koori women in White feminist issues. (Felton and Flanagan, 1993:58)

They see the community as something to be sustained and protected, and therefore a touchstone for their politics:

> We have to draw on the strengths and ideas of our whole community to get a balanced perception. Self determination and community control is what we are striving for. This can only be obtained if we develop a strong sense of identity . . . We must promote the value of extended families and kinship ties and above all retain our sense of community. (ibid.:59)

Ruby Langford Ginibi evokes various communities in her storytelling. She describes *Don't Take Your Love to Town* as a story of Aboriginal motherhood: 'I did that in nearly every chapter in this book, I mean, give birth . . . and I will say, this is not only my book, my story, it's the story of every Aboriginal woman in this country today that's got kids to raise' (Langford, 1994a:114). She also describes her book as the story of five generations, from her father's father—Sam Anderson—to her grandchildren. The extended family, as an integral aspect of the itinerant lifestyle of Langford and other Aborigines, is very much both the context and the subject of her narrative. Langford's immediate family in *Don't Take Your Love to Town* moves between the rural and urban districts of New South Wales, Victoria and Queensland. A nomadic lifestyle such as this, necessitated by the availability of work and the needs and demands of relatives, is sustained by a complex of communities.

On a number of occasions Langford describes cohabitation as a necessity for both economic and emotional reasons. And although, as Tim Rowse notes, her narrative bears evidence of the rupturing, decline and breakdown of kin networks (Rowse, 1993a; 1993b), I would argue that Langford's network nevertheless survives and sustains both her and her children. For although the 'deculturation' through urbanisation of Aboriginal people is often seen as having a negative effect on kin networks, there is ample evidence of their survival in both rural and urban environments in *Don't Take Your Love to Town*. This is even more marked in *My Bundjalung People* where, after many years' absence, Langford reaffirms her links with family and friends and is able to identify exactly how they are related to her; 'this world is getting smaller by the minute', she says (Langford, 1994c:174).

Langford describes living at Katoomba as 'a healthy life but isolated—not enough Kooris to go around' (Langford, 1988:126); hence her decision to move back to an inner-city area. She had the same problem with the Housing Commission house in Green Valley, and she criticises the government's policy of integration for 'splitting up the Aboriginal communities' (ibid.:176). The Commission's regulation against extended families living in the same house was a re-enactment of the monitoring and surveillance of Aborigines in the missions. It violated a central aspect of Aboriginal life, namely that 'survival often depended on being able to stay with friends and relatives' (ibid.:174). Elsewhere she says, 'I always had a houseful wherever I went. It was a means of survival' (ibid.:158). She talks about survival here in both the economic and emotional senses. Towards the end of the narrative, several men in her extended family—such as her brother Kevin, and her son Nobby— fight to maintain the will to survive: Kevin loses this battle, and Nobby often seems close to losing it too. Langford's other two sons, David and Jeff, also struggle periodically with depression. The men in her family seem particularly vulnerable to emotional and psychological devastation (see her further comments on this subject—Langford, 1994d:81). O'Shane similarly comments that the apparent strength of Aboriginal women can belie the sometimes more traumatic effects of racism on Aboriginal men (O'Shane, 1976:32).

If Langford's narratives testify to the power of resistant Aboriginal communities, they are written with the express purpose of raising the consciousness of white Australians. Sommer makes the point that Latin American women's *testimonios* have a political agenda: 'they are written neither for individual growth nor for glory but are offered through the scribe to a broad public as one part of a general strategy to win political ground' (Sommer, 1988:109). Langford's narratives have a clear educative agenda. In work-in-progress on her son's biography, she says: 'That's what I keep bumping my gums about! . . . Trying to educate people with my talks about conditions [of poverty in which her family lives]' (Langford, 1994b:55). She sees her role of writer and speaker as a professional one and humorously underlines her role as an educator after a conversation with some people about her country: '"just leave my lecturing fee on the counter"', she says as she leaves (Langford, 1994c:206). It is important, then, that we read Aboriginal women's life-histories not just as autobiography in the literary sense, but as evidence of knowledges shaped by gender and race. Langford suggests, for example, that her narratives should be studied in schools not only as literature but as history (Langford, 1994d:80). Like many of the Aboriginal women quoted earlier (pp. 56–64), Langford prefers to describe her auto- and biographical narratives as 'history'. She is suspicious of the label 'fiction' and its implied opposition to 'truth' (1994a:102, 109). (On the other hand, Doris Pilkington preferred the medium of fiction in her first book, *Caprice: A Stockman's Daughter*, which was based only in part on her mother's life.) Extensive debates about taxonomising minority women's autobiographical narratives (e.g. Davies, 1992; Kaplan, 1992, both discussed above, pp. 64–6) lose some of their relevance in light of Aboriginal women's stated preference for the term 'history', although Carole Ferrier's argument that classifying Aboriginal women's autobiographical narratives as novels may be politically strategic in introducing them into literature courses has some merit (Ferrier, 1992).

Aboriginal women's life (hi)stories construct alternative versions of self and community that resist and oppose the hegemonic narratives of individualism and nationalism. At a time when both capitalism and the state continue to appropriate signifiers of

Aboriginality for discourses of popular nationalism, Aboriginal women's texts can be seen as opposing homogenisation by modes of self-narration and a re-reading of the past that resist the collapse and absorption of difference.

'Aboriginality' is a useful notion in mobilising alternative readings of Aboriginal texts. Aboriginal people are possibly the most researched demographic group in Australia (Daylight and Johnstone, 1986:1), and have always been managed and administered as a racial category (Pettman, 1992b:19); Marcia Langton underlines the proliferation of the discourse of naming Aborigines when she points out (quoting John McCorquordale) that there are sixty-seven definitions of Aboriginal people in Australian law (Langton, 1994:96). As a discourse of race, Aboriginality is a useful counter-discourse to the rhetoric of white administration. In Aboriginal women's auto-biographical narratives, gender and class issues also impinge upon and interrupt discourses of race. Key aspects of the Aboriginality of women's autobiographical narratives include their oral nature and their roots in specific communities. Here story-telling is principally a performative practice. The stories told are part of larger repertoires that the tellers draw upon and adapt according to their various purposes and the needs of different audiences. As Davies observes, stories exist 'in multiple forms, not necessarily locked into writing as a finite form in the way we see it in the academy' (Davies, 1992:8).

Because their own relationship to the past is complex, story-tellers mediate between their present circumstances and the desire to communicate an experience of that past (P. Hamilton, 1990:131). The 'truth' and 'authenticity' of such memories will depend on the social and political specificities of the speaker's own enunciative position. These stories do not necessarily reveal the past 'as it actually was'. As self-conscious and performative acts of self-dramatisation, they show rather how it is retold. As Paula Hamilton suggests, 'the invention of the particular self in the oral form . . . [is] a form of acting; a fictional performance of self' (ibid.:130). Sidonie Smith (1994:3) reminds us that there is a slippage between the speaker, the narrator and the subject of the narration; these tensions vary in both oral performance and reading, thus constituting varying subjectivities. How Aboriginal people make narratives of the past relates to the way they constitute themselves in the present, and those enunciative sites are never fixed. Each reciting is a re-siting of the self. Collectively they recall different moments in history, and constitute different socio-political sites of Aboriginality in the present. As Judith Butler argues, a political signifier of identity is 'a non-representational term whose semantic emptiness becomes the occasion for a set of phantasmatic investments to accrue . . . which . . . wields the power to rally and mobilise, indeed to produce the very political constituency it appears to "represent"' (Butler, 1993:199). It is as necessary to invoke political identities, she suggests, as to recognise their provisionality. This performative notion of Aboriginality echoes Spivak's advocacy of 'strategic essentialism' in conditions where strategy changes moment to moment (Spivak, 1993:13). It contrasts with those reified and com-modified signifiers of Aboriginality in white nationalist discourse, which present Aboriginality as something fixed and resolved (and also with an excessively cautious hesitation over essentialism; see, for example, Hollinsworth, 1992; Lattas, 1992). Aboriginality, as Langton reminds us, arises from the intersubjectivity of black and white people; before the arrival of white invaders there was no Aboriginality in the sense that it is meant today. It arises from an intercultural dialogue and is constantly remade as relations between black and white Australians change (Langton, 1994:98–9).

## Aboriginal autobiographical narratives in the arena of post-colonial studies

The narrativisation of Aboriginal women's memories, that is, their transformation into formal narrative, contributes to the project of making visible the otherwise invisible history of the colonisation of Australia's indigenous peoples, and to the reinscribing and renaming of decolonised space. It is important that these spaces are not recodified, recolonised and appropriated by white discourses. As Foucault points out, buried and disguised 'historical contents' can be accessed by criticism, but because other subjugated knowledges —'naive knowledges'—are popular, they exist outside 'the hierarchy of knowledges and sciences'. They are 'naive' not in a patronising sense but because they embody extra-cognitive and extra-scientistic local and popular practices. It is important, therefore, that those 'naive knowledges' transmitted through story-telling be not subsumed and coerced by the dominant culture into a 'theoretical, unitary, formal and scientific discourse' (Foucault, 1980:85). In order to avoid recodifying such knowledges and practices as sciences, we must be attentive to their local and gendered characteristics, that is, to the social and contingent nature of their utterances. By bringing this genealogy to bear on the teaching of Aboriginal women's texts, we can avoid depoliticising and aestheticising.

The discourse of post-colonialism, which was designed in opposition to such practices, has itself become so universalising as to be open to criticisms on those grounds. Ella Shohat, for example, questions 'ahistorical and universalizing deployments' of the terms 'post-colonial' and 'post-colonialism' and their 'potentially depoliticizing implications' (Shohat, 1992:99). Since the 'post' in post-colonial suggests something coming 'after' a colonialism which has ended, the term is imbued with 'an ambiguous spatio-temporality' (ibid.:102). It collapses the difference between the colonised and colonising 'settlers' and the colonised indigenous populations of the 'settler'-states. The term 'post-colonial' is therefore unhelpful when talking about Aboriginal constituencies. Carrying implications that colonialism is a matter of the past, it 'leaves no space . . . for the struggles of aboriginals in Australia' (ibid. :105). Shohat argues for 'a more nuanced discourse' in which the concept of the post-colonial is 'interrogated and contextualized historically, geo-politically and culturally', a discourse which will 'address the politics of location' (ibid.:108, 111, 112).

Other theorists have followed the same line of reasoning. Hugh Webb, for example, thinks that post-colonial, 'as a framing discursive marker for Aboriginal culture' is 'a confused misnomer' (Webb, 1991:32). Mishra and Hodge argue that 'an uncritical adulation of pluralism . . . leads, finally, to postcolonialism becoming the liberal Australian version of multiculturalism'. They conclude with the recommendation that 'smaller *récits* must replace the *grand récit* of postcolonialism . . . so that we can know the historical background better. In these smaller *récits* it may well be that the term "post-colonial" is never used' (Mishra and Hodge, 1991:410, 412).

The proliferation of Aboriginal women's autobiographies is part of the complex process that is transforming contemporary Australian culture. These narratives have had a marked effect on white cultural amnesia, and have exemplified Benedict Anderson's dictum that a country's biography, 'because it can not be "remembered", must be narrated' (Anderson, 1991:204). Aboriginal renarrativisations of the past, however, should not be recuperated by the white discourses of nationalism. White Australia is passing through ever more nuanced phases of neo-colonialism. The more visible Aboriginal culture becomes, the greater the danger that it will be appropriated and commodified by the dominant white culture into which it is inserted.

Although Aboriginal people continue to engage in practices of decolonisation, the post-colonial moment is necessarily inscribed in utopian trajectories. In Spivak's words, however, 'postcolonialism doesn't exist', for it 'assumes that decolonization has taken place. A more appropriate question is who decolonizes?' (Spivak, 1991:75). In other words, it is politically more useful to foreground the process of decolonisation than to foreclose this complex and contestatory process by using the term 'post-colonialism'.

To explore the process of decolonisation as articulated in Aboriginal women's autobiographies is in accord with Mishra and Hodge's recommendation that the objects of our attention should be small rather than grand or totalising *récits*. This process is productive and generative. Following Foucault, I would describe the emergent *récits* in these Aboriginal women's narratives as marking the insurrection of 'subjugated' and 'naive' knowledges. If we remind ourselves of the oral traditions in which the story-telling features of Aboriginal women's autobiographies originated, we can recognise the social and counselling role played by such knowledges. As Heather Goodall suggests, the circumstances in which Aboriginal people share their memories are critical (Goodall, 1987:29). By keeping in mind the contingent and performative act of story-telling we can thus avoid depoliticising and aestheticising these stories.

# 4

# Nationalism and Globalism: Ania Walwicz

Issues of identity, representation and subjectivity are similarly problematised by migrant and diasporic subjects. The situation of these subjects calls for a theoretical practice that is deconstructive but also sympathetic to strategic constructions of identity and informed by feminist notions of subjectivity. Diasporic feminists like Spivak and Trinh take their cue from Julia Kristeva in defining their feminism as a negative cultural practice. According to Kristeva,

> a feminist practice can only be negative, at odds with what already exists so that we may say 'that's not it' and 'that's still not it.' In 'woman' I see something that cannot be represented, something that is not said, something above and beyond nomenclatures and ideologies. (Kristeva, 1986:137)

Spivak and Trinh are less concerned with identifying an originary female consciousness than with deconstructing patriarchal and First World feminist constructions of women and the colonised subject. They criticise liberal feminism for ignoring the specificities of class and race in its construction of gender (Spivak, 1987:255–7). Yet in spite of persistently questioning and bringing into crisis the notion of subjectivity (specifically with reference to the subaltern, or the disenfranchised or subordinate classes), Spivak concedes that 'the intellectual's solution'—and the same might be said also of the minority subject—'is not to abstain from representation' (Spivak, 1988:285). She highlights the predicament of the radical intellectual, who is caught between 'granting to the oppressed either that very expressive subjectivity which s/he criticizes or, instead, a total unrepresentability' (Spivak, 1987:209). She goes on to say that in order to negotiate this opposition it is necessary to position the subaltern subject provisionally. Taking the work of the Subaltern Studies group (a collection of intellectuals based in India, Australia and the UK whose work is inspired by Gramsci's discussion of the politics of subaltern classes) as an exemplary case, Spivak approves their use of 'subject-restoration' as 'crucially strategic':

> the project to retrieve the subaltern consciousness [is] the attempt to undo a massive historiographic metalepsis and 'situate' the effect of the subject as subaltern. I would read it, then, as a *strategic* use of positivist essentialism in a scrupulously visible political interest. (ibid.:209, 205)

The problem of how to enable the subaltern to speak is symptomatic of a larger crisis in representation: 'the historical predicament of the colonial subaltern can be made to become the allegory of the predicament of *all* thought, *all* deliberative consciousness' (ibid.:204). The need to make strategic use of essentialism is equally symptomatic of our contemporary condition: 'claiming a *positive* subject-position for the subaltern might be reinscribed as a strategy for our times' (ibid.:207).

## Ethnicity and postmodernism

If Aboriginal identity is defined by race, the other minority constituency managed by the discourse of nationality in Australia— the 'multicultural'—is defined by ethnicity. As Marie de Lepervanche (1980) shows, the discourse of racism in relation to non-indigenous people was replaced by that of ethnicity after the influx into Australia of immigrant labour after World War II, and specifically with the introduction of a mass migration programme in 1947. Because Australia needed both labour and consumers, it encouraged 'settler' migration rather than guestworkers (Bottomley, 1992:151). This meant that immigrants found Australian citizenship relatively easy to attain, at least from the 1970s onwards, albeit through a process of 'naturalisation' (Pettman, 1992b:39).

From 1947 to 1973 immigrant labour provided 50 per cent of labour-force growth, thus giving Australia the highest rate of increase of any OECD country (Castles and Miller, 1993:74). Changing circumstances in the structural relations between labour and capital resulted in new cultural manifestations, institutions and forms. These in turn prompted new policies, such as the dropping of the so-called White Australia policy in 1965 (Foster and Stockley, 1984:54), the introduction of the Racial Discrimination Act in 1975, and various multicultural policy statements since 1978 (ibid.:90). Andrew Jakubowicz argues that nationalist constructions of multiculturalism officially came into being in order to manage a racially segmented work-force, and that the state mobilised the discourse of ethnicity in the general interests of capital. The loyalties activated by appeals to ethnic cultural bonds were utilised to sustain social order and productivity. Multiculturalism is thus a strategy to reconstruct and to sustain the established power bloc (Jakubowicz, 1984). Since 1947 there has been a continuous policy of planned immigration, designed to increase both the population and economic growth (Castles and Miller, 1993:99). This has been managed since the late 1970s by policies of multiculturalism which deploy the concept of ethnicity. As a result, ethnicity has emerged as a new social category as significant as that of class (de Lepervanche, 1980:29).

The discourse of multiculturalism promulgates the concept of cultural diversity, which defines ethnicity according to visible, folk-markers of difference. Issues of power differentials between and within minority groups are thereby obscured. The American model of liberal pluralism which informs Australian multiculturalism policy has been critiqued for reifying difference into stereotypic models of identity. Multiculturalism, as a process in the construction of social knowledge, naturalises identity, making it a matter of biology, history or culture rather than 'the effect of an enunciation of difference that constitutes hierarchies and asymmetries of power' (Scott, 1992:14).

In order to rethink difference, we need to move away from discourses that construct identity as pre-social, primordial or socio-biologically determined. Following Homi Bhabha, theorists have foregrounded difference as a process of enunciation and significa-tion, and have focused on 'the discontinuous, intertextual temporality of cultural difference' (Bhabha, 1988:22). Such constructions of cultural difference in turn articulate 'national, anti-nationalistic histories of the people' (ibid.). Stuart Hall, for example, argues for a 'new ethnicity' that, like Bhabha's notion of cultural difference, will generate a counter-discourse to nationalism. Echoing Spivak's claim that the crisis in representing the subaltern is allegorical of a general crisis in notions of representation, Hall contends that both the migrant and the colonised exemplify the postmodern experience of a de-centered subjectivity. Black identity, he suggests, has 'always been an unstable identity, psychically, culturally and politically' (Hall, 1987:45). Hall goes on to argue that 'narratives of displacement' (ibid.) cannot be left completely unresolved, for without moments of closure (however arbitrary and contingent) neither a sense of identity nor a politics could be formed. Without closure, however provisional or temporary, we would be stuck with the 'infinite semiosis of meaning' and 'infinite dispersal' (ibid.) On this point he distances himself from postmodernism, claiming that 'the politics of infinite dispersal is the politics of no action at all' (ibid.).

Michael M. J. Fischer develops the idea of ethnicity in postmodern times by linking it to memory. He emphasises the dynamics of ethnicity as 'something reinvented and reinterpreted each generation by each individual' (Fischer, 1986:195). Reinvention is enabled by remembering. Because it is constantly in a process of renewing human values, ethnic memory is oriented to the future, not the past (ibid.:201; see also Hatzimanolis, 1993:139). I will return shortly to the roles of memory and history in the invention of ethnicity. In the meantime it is useful to explore this notion of a dynamic and reinvented ethnicity with the assistance of Judith Butler's concept of performativity. For what results is a conception of 'performative ethnicity' that can be applied to a reading of *red roses*, the third book by the Polish-Australian writer, Ania Walwicz.

Judith Butler argues that gender, as an identity, is not stable but rather 'instituted through a stylised repetition of acts' (Butler, 1990a:270). The 'possibilities of gender transformation', she goes on, 'are to be found in the arbitrary relation between such acts, in the possibility of a different sort of repeating, in the breaking or subversive repetition of that style' (ibid.:271). Butler uses the word 'act' in the sense of 'bodily gestures, movements, and enactments of various kinds' (ibid.:270). The concept of repetitive performative acts, however, can be mobilised in the arena of speech and writing, and in the construction not only of gender but of ethnicity. The spatiality of representation (that is, the way subjectivity occupies space, both technically and discursively) is challenged in *red roses* by what Judith Butler calls the 'social temporality' of gender and ethnicity (ibid.:271). Instead of being fixed in the regulatory fictions of binary oppositions and stereotypes, gender and ethnicity can be seen in terms of performative acts—temporal rather than spatial, or (in Michel de Certeau's terms) tactical rather than strategic. Butler suggests that 'performance may preempt narrative as the scene of gender production' (Butler, 1990b:339). Although *red roses* is indisputably a narrative and not a performance, it is a narrative interrupted constantly by its collage-like composition which foregrounds the oral and performative nature of language.

As Hall suggests, identity has always been unstable for migrants and minority groups. The self that Walwicz constructs through dramatisation in *red roses* is self-reflexive and performative: it interrogates the notion of representation, and parodies the received discourses it imitates and quotes. *red roses* is a fabrication of the self that names itself as such. Its principal trope is imitation and mimicry, a strategy characteristic of colonised and minority peoples (Bhabha, 1994). The narratorial voice is constantly shifting within a large range of registers. These include the ventriloquising of famous 'people', such as film stars, historical figures (e.g. Hitler), Disney cartoon characters (e.g. Mickey Mouse), and the collage-like 'quotation' of a wide variety of written texts. Mimicry and quotation establish the text's theatrical quality. The polyphonic voice evokes a theatre of famous figures, a repertoire of 'actors' (past and present) drawn from the narrator's own life. The narrator says: 'i am getting ready the scenario the inevitable play script the necessary language i am monsieur and she is countess' (Walwicz, 1992a:58); 'i speak behind a mask', she adds (ibid.:88). These small theatrical 'scenarios' are scattered through the text. The narrative voice—split into multiple voices—delays closure, and conjures up a sense of identity through an accumulation and shuffling of fragments.

This sense of voice as theatre foregrounds language as perform-ance. 'All statements are performative', the narrator tells us and, 'it's not what is said it's in the way of telling' (ibid.:119, 130). The notion of the self as something performed through language is explored principally in the notion of gender. Gender 'roles' are epitomised by various film stars, whose voices and images the narrator appropriates in order to fabricate the absent mother, and (through that metaphor) the self. Ethnicity, like gender, is seen as a historical assemblage of performances. The narrator traces, for example, the diasporic trajectories of transformative Jewish ethnicity:

> the jews in france adopting all the grace but they're originally from poland the photographs of jews looking very french just like the french the photographs of jews looking very fair and aryan the photographs of jews looking very jewish but they're not french then who are you either or or what she was she said i had enough of that then i had enough of it all i had enough of the whole thing then i was done with that i was done with it all i was done with i was i wanted to have nothing more to do with them or it or me at all i was done with and done i didn't want it any longer i wanted just to get away . . . tired of having to be just myself i wanted to be other people too i had enough of it i wanted to be end with all that i wanted to be done with it i wanted to invent myself and make myself apart and to be what i wanted i was overburdened with all that history of the town i wanted to be done with all that i wanted to begin just today. (ibid.:175–6)

This passage—together with two 'prose clusters' ('new world' and 'Poland') from her first book, *writing*—traces the diasporic trajectory from the old world to the new. Two points are of interest here: the mutability and lability of ethnicity, and the rejection of history. Through diaspora the burden of history is discarded, and the self is remade anew and 'apart' from the past; she 'begin[s] just today'. Walwicz describes her writing, however, as a 'record' (Walwicz, n.d.[a]:14). In documenting both her own experience and fragments of family history, her project involves not only forgetting but also recollecting, recording and rewriting the past. Paradoxically, it reinvents the very discourse it seeks to abandon, namely history. I will return to this point later.

## The performative voice

If the Jew epitomises the diasporic mutability of ethnicity, it is through the mother that the narrator traces the genealogy of a gender intimately intertwined with ethnicity. The mother is a complex feature in *red roses*: she is 'the enormous the gigantic a symbol' (ibid.:213). The text is a journey back through memory and history to retrieve the mother, but also to stage a cathartic release from her. It is worth exploring how the mother functions in the performative and enunciative staging of the narrative voice.

In *red roses* the voice becomes a stage upon which the theatre of ethnic and gender identity is played out. The mother is the muse invoked by the narrative voice in the vocative case—'droga mamo' ('dear mum') (ibid.:3). The act of writing a letter to the mother is repeated several times (ibid.:14, 74, 105, 149, 206). The narrator frequently exhorts the mother to reply. 'Will you send me aletter [sic] or a telegram will you tell me . . . your address your telegram number', she asks; 'please return my letters' (ibid.:2, 3). In one sense, there can be no response from the mother, for the process of writing is an invocation of an absent addressee or muse. Writing epitomises the paradox at the heart of representation, namely that the referents—what the words refer to—are always absent. The journey in search of the mother (or referent) can therefore never reach its destination. The mother thus symbolises the referent that can never be fully realised in language. She is as spectral as her 'talk': 'she is saying me now the phantom talk of mum the ghost' (ibid.:11). Paradoxically, language (like memory) 'speaks' from the absence it speaks about.

None the less, the mother is the enabling condition of the text, and as muse inspires the narrator's enunciation. The relationship between muse and narrator is dialogic: the narrator speaks (to) the mother/text, which in turn 'speaks' her. The personification of the mother highlights the social and dialogic nature of writing by exposing the dynamics of the relationship between addresser and addressee. *red roses* is described as a diary (ibid.:186). Elsewhere Walwicz has talked about the genesis of her writing in diaries, and how even diary-writing presupposes an addressee (Walwicz, 1992b:828). Although the keeping of a diary would appear to epitomise a solitary and intransitive practice of writing, Walwicz describes it as 'cathartic' and 'magical' (ibid.:829). *red roses* engenders an alchemical reaction between addresser and addressee by addressing the mother directly and exhorting her to reply. The interrogatory and exhortative mode of address creates a sense of dialogue. Speech and writing become transaction or theatre, that is, the enactment of a verbal event which calls the self into being. In *red roses* these fundamentally social acts of exchange and transformation may take place on either a psychological or a somatic or bodily level. Walwicz has described how reading can engender a physiological identification with the author (P. Rose, 1994:78).

As the initial addressee of *red roses*, the mother is therefore the vehicle of narratorial transformation. This takes place across a number of sites, variously designated as the mother or the anonymous 'she'. We can see this movement in the following self-reflexive passage, which suggests that writing is always 'a relationship of more than one', a circular and alchemical process which returns the narrator to herself. This passage also suggests that the addressee of *red roses* is split, and in fact can be either 'someone' or 'her' (the mother): 'who do you write for mainly myself and herself this is talking to someone then to her and to me a relationship now of more than one or lonely this is a talk about my mother' (Walwicz, 1992a:206).

The doubling of the mother with the anonymous 'she' results in a concertina effect, facilitated in *red roses* by a slippage between the pronouns 'she/her' and 'you'. Although the mother is generally positioned as the addressee of the text, the pronouns 'she/her' and 'you' are rarely attached to a proper name, and clearly invoke more than one particular woman. Often the lack of differentiation between these women collapses them back into the mother: 'i am writing a letter to you i am writing a letter to mother' (ibid.:14). At other times the movement is in the opposite direction, and other women are generated by the indeterminacy of the address to the mother. The narrator makes this point succinctly when she says: 'i substitute one woman for another woman' (ibid.:170). A dual process of collapse and proliferation therefore takes place throughout the text. And so when the narrator adopts the persona of the mother ('i am writing a letter to my daughter but she won't answer' [ibid.:85]), it is the mother who 'speaks' the daughter. While the writing is staged as a dialogue with an absent woman, ultimately it is a 'conversation' with or representation of oneself: 'she is writing letters to herself' (ibid.:14). Writing is a transformative and/or cathartic performance of self.

Walwicz draws attention to the dynamics of positioning in the act of enunciation. She parodies the epistolary or letter-writing convention of constructing a first-person narrator: one long sequence begins as a letter to the narrator's mother before turning into a love letter, a letter breaking an engagement, a legal letter, a sympathy letter, a thank-you letter, a letter of introduction, and so on (ibid.:145–7). This collage of phrases foregrounds the generic conventionality of written communication. It also makes clear which rules Walwicz is breaking in this text. Opening the sequence with the statement, 'the sentence can be the beginner no pause of a break' (ibid.:45), she draws attention not only to her delegitimation of the sentence as the basic unit of written communication, but also to her own reworking of 'pause' and 'break' into a language which she describes as 'the notation and enactment of states of feeling/being' (Walwicz, 1992b:819). The sequence concludes with the statement that 'excessive punctuation tends to destroy the flow of a piece of writing' (Walwicz, 1992a:147), a rule of grammar which Walwicz pushes to its extreme.

The constant address to the mother engenders a strong sense of the oral transaction and performativity of language. The narrator tells us that she is 'eavesdrop and listening and hearing' (ibid.:122), and that she is garnering her voices from the world around her. This orality in turn evokes the body. There are many references to both the mouth and language as exchange, as found text (ibid.:58), as something we borrow or steal from other people. This process is exemplified in the art of the collage-maker and the *bricoleuse* (who can make things out of whatever materials are available), and never comes to us except by way of someone else: 'you have a way with words they get into my mouth' (ibid.:88). The act of exchanging words is a focal one in the text: the mother often exchanges words by singing. Her words are also likened to blood in the mouth, milk or food (ibid.:1–3, 108, 144, 30), evoking the pre-Oedipal relationship with the maternal body. Language is seen not as an aspect of that paternal law described by Jacques Lacan, but as having a somatic origin as the expression of the infant's physical bond with the mother's body. Other women in the text evoke this bond with the maternal body, and facilitate language in the same way that the mother does: 'you talk her through my trance mouth' (ibid.:5).

By focusing on language as performance—that is, on its oral and theatrical aspects—the narrative of *red roses* foregrounds the power of language to fascinate and seduce. Story-telling and the fairy-tale have pride of place in this narrative. The magician becomes a metaphor for the writer, whose practice is likened to invention and make believe (ibid.:131, 128, 105). The writer is a magician and trickster, inventing childhoods, life stories, and identities: 'i am becoming another self and another person she plays me' (ibid.:179). Language, like memory, is unreliable and illusory. The narrator is both a stealer of other people words (ibid.:74) and a liar (ibid.:9, 26, 68). She is also unreliable: 'i am becoming devious and indirect and discreet i'm not tell you everything' (ibid.:127). Reading the narrative is like solving a riddle or unwinding threads (ibid.:120). Because it lacks linearity and plot, the collage-narrative of *red roses* is inconclusive and open ended. Like the folk-story (ibid.:85), it is made up of repetitions with variations, and 'never ends'. In the case of collage, as with memory, 'there's always everything unfinished' (ibid.:140). Ethnicity and gender are a collage-like assemblage of performative acts and choices; they are open ended and unfinished.

This emphasis on language as performance, and on the self as an ensemble of different voices, points to the fact that performance exceeds knowledge. For as Spivak would have it, 'what is known is always in excess of knowledge. Knowledge is never adequate to its object' (Spivak, 1987:254). The activation of voices in an open-ended collage produces 'a whole composed of parts and bigger than the parts' (Walwicz, 1992a:58). In the telling of the story, meaning proliferates: 'i'm all telling by not telling in that way i tell more and more than i even know' (ibid.:147). As the narrator points out, this type of text clearly involves the reader in a highly participative role:

i just outline a sketch you never reveal her completely or yourself why do should i you have to make her up i'm just giving suggestions i don't want to say completely and fully i'm just hinting at a story then you just read me carefully the reader participates the reader reads the reader makes me. (ibid.:115–16)

The narrator's playfulness, which introduces uncertainty into the process of making sense of the text, is essentially seductive, although this is not a passive experience for the reader. The reading of a verbal collage is highly performative and participative, because the syntactical breaks produce ambiguities that result in polysemousness, or multiple meanings. In bridging the gaps and dislocations of the text we actively make sense of it in the same way that we construct memory or history.

## Collage

Walwicz personifies language as the mother, who is a metaphor for the crisis of representation and identity. Originary notions of identity are replaced in *red roses* with ideas of fabrication and constructedness: 'i didn't have a mother i am making one up here to . . . fill a gap a void i am making up i am making mum talk' (ibid.:32). When the narrator says, 'i'm just making myself from her and many other things' (ibid.:206), she signals the arbitrary nature of the way we construct our origins. The text's fabrication of the mother draws on the techniques of collage: 'i am sticking toget her [sic] i am attaching with glue out of bits i am making a mother' (ibid.:12). (The glue image is particularly resonant, since the French word *collage* means 'gluing' or 'pasting'.) Memory's *modus operandi* could be said to be that of collage, in so far as the narrator constructs the mother from fragments of language: 'i am making up a mother a biography out of what's said' (ibid.:79). The collage-structure of *red roses* is most obvious in Walwicz's fractured syntax, and in her abandonment of punctuation as a means of organising sentences.

The narrative of *red roses* invites us to read the constellated imagery of the absent mother as a metaphor of the self which, like the mother, must be fabricated and 'stuck together' from fragments of memory and history. This process negates the idea of an originary self, and therefore of an originary ethnicised or gendered identity. But collage generally also works against the reterritorialising effect of metaphor, which re-encodes meaning. The paratactic structure—placing one clause after another without traditional grammatical links—of *red roses* generally militates against reading its images as symbols or metaphors (Hazel Smith, 1989:7). The reiterative parallelism of the disrupted syntax, together with a lack of conjunctive and linking structures, produces a layering effect. This is not a rhetoric of convergence or condensation, which Lacan sees as definitive of metaphor, but rather of the displacement characteristic of metonymy and synecdoche (Lacan, 1966). This is particularly clear in the synecdochic imagery of the body, which evokes somatic flows and desires. The discontinuities of the collage-textuality of Walwicz's writing—with its parataxis and repetitions—militates against the kind of metaphoric readings produced in response to lyric poetry or realist prose. Walwicz's strategy, by contrast, is to re-literalise language. This is not to argue that metaphor and symbol are entirely absent from a writer who refers to her 'wardrobe of particular symbols' (Walwicz, 1992b:825). But the reiterative permutations of phrases and images in the collage-like composition of *red roses* resist symbolist notions of depth and metaphoricity, and are more amenable to a postmodernist interest in the flatness and surfaces of words.

At another level, *red roses* is a discursive collage. The discourses of childhood erupt into the text in the form of songs, fairy-stories, folk-tales, television cartoons, comics and nursery rhymes. Other discourses originate in the media (especially advertising and journalese) or in literary genres such as the detective novel, the romance novel, biographies of film stars, literature, and literary theory. Still others come from pornography, tour guides, phrasebooks, grammar books, women's magazines, science writing, travel diaries, gardening, cooking and dieting. Linguistically, *red roses* is a collage of French, German and Polish snippets. This multilingualism creates what the narrator (borrowing from Dadaism) calls 'wordy salads' (Walwicz, 1992a:77). As this image suggests, the purpose of collage is not to unify fragments into a coherent and seamless whole, but to allow them to maintain their alterity within the composition. The effect is randomness and dislocation. Collage encourages a double reading: the fragment is read in terms of both its original and its new context (Perloff, 1986:47). In collage, intertextuality reigns: 'everything refers a reference' (Walwicz, 1992a:181). By means of pastiche and mimicry, collage promotes the play of difference and avoids establishing a hierarchy of discourses by refusing to privilege any of them. Pastiche and mimicry are strategies characteristic of women, for whom femininity is essentially a masquerade (Rivière, 1986). They are practised also by minority people whose experience of the dominant discourse is mediated and relativised. Collage reminds us that meaning and representation are unstable, temporary, relative and provisional. The collage-like textuality of *red roses* foregrounds discontinuity—between cultures, between childhood and adulthood, and between received representations and the performative aspect of gender and ethnicity.

In collage, words are *objets trouvés*—found objects—rather than moments of originary consciousness. The modes of detachment, readherence, grafting and citation evince a world knowable only in terms of representation, constructedness, and the intertextuality of language. Collage thus exemplifies the condition of the diasporic, the migrant, the exile, the refugee, the cosmopolite and the traveller. In this light, *red roses* can be read as a travel diary, a journal, or the sort of map that Steven Connor calls a 'periplus', which marks out a journey one step at a time rather than providing an overview (Connor, 1989:227–8). The narrative of *red roses* is not subject to chronological linearity. Instead it mimics the fragmentary and discontinuous nature of memory and history.

Each of these three genres—the travel diary, journal and map, plus the ancillary genres of tourist guide and phrase-book—is invoked in Walwicz's narrative, which slips from place to place (Perth, Sydney, Melbourne, Singapore, Paris, Germany, the USA, England, Ireland, Italy, Japan and Poland). The journey is a dominant motif. 'I am preparing journeys and maps', the narrator announces; 'i have reisen [sic] fieber the fever of travel i am going away soon'; and later she mentions writing 'in my travel diary in my diary of travels' (Walwicz, 1992a:98, 94, 186). The narrative *mélange* (or mix), which rarely provides any preamble to a change of setting, invokes the shifting, fluid world of both memory and of the traveller. The narrator's 'lack of a solid world' (ibid.:206) suggests not only the traveller's sense of rootlessness but also the shifting and intertextual nature of representation and signification.

The journey is also a motif in the context of reading as a process or passage. The image of the (un)winding thread appears several times, and becomes a metaphor for the seduction of the reader. An extended passage begins with images of ravioli and a jumper unravelling; it proceeds, in a style reminiscent of magic realism, to follow the thread around table and chairs, through a room, a dance, and so on. Here the thread clearly symbolises the narrative we try to follow, teased by a narrator who asks cheekily, 'where's the story now answer a comprehension test' (ibid.:66). 'I'm just a fascinator', she confesses. Hence her prescription: 'read me slow' (ibid.:65).

The most sustained use of the journey motif is that of the pilgrimage to the mother. It is a journey into the past and into memory, mapped in the non-linear mode of collage: rhizomatic—growing outwards, fragmented and episodic, like language and memory:

> i am trying to solve a riddle or unwind a thread the signs are not systematic they are all intermittent they are flashing on and off i am using an absence in my code a langue i am a signwriter of a sign i am not the i the writer i am just my mum and mums i'm a memory now a flashback. (ibid.:120)

The pilgrimage to the mother is also a 'reverse jurney' [sic] from the past and memory into the present and language. These are symbolised respectively by the umbilical cord ('a knot in my stomach') attaching her to the mother and by 'a typewriter ribbon' (ibid.:207).

Textually, the collage of *red roses* can be said to evoke the relativity of representation. But it also articulates the political strategy —familiar to migrants and minority constituencies—of reinscribing oneself not in terms of a fixed identity (such as the originary, nativist or ethnicist discourse of multiculturalism) but through mimicry and pastiche of dominant representations. Constructing a collage from these fragments of discourse, the writer can forsake the fixed and limiting borders of the multicultural nation, and inhabit instead the dislocated world of the traveller and the vagrant. Paul Carter (1992) identifies collage as a defining characteristic of the 'migrant aesthetic'. He defines post-colonial Australia as 'a migrant society', because the majority of its population are 'settlers' and immigrants who historically have never had a common language. The 'migrant self' inhabits what he calls an 'artefactual reality' (Carter, 1992:198), made up linguistically and visually out of heterogeneous elements reproduced imitatively and parodically. In the post-colonial and 'settler' environment of Australia, Carter argues, collage is 'the normal mode of constructing meaning' (ibid.:187).

## History, memory, archive

In the diasporic trajectory from the old world to the new, the burden of history appears to have been discarded, and the self remade anew. And yet Walwicz's project in *red roses* is to recollect and rewrite the past. It is useful at this point to bear in mind Maurice Halbwachs's distinction between two different sorts of memory, 'autobiographical memory' and 'historical memory'. The former comprises events we have experienced personally; the latter, those we hear or read about:

> During my life, my national society has been theater for a number of events that I say I 'remember,' events that I know about only from newspapers or the testimony of those directly involved. These events occupy a place in the memory of the nation, but I myself did not witness them. In recalling them, I must rely entirely upon the memory of others . . . I often know such events no better nor in any other manner than I know historical events that occurred before I was born. I carry a baggage load of historical remembrances that I can increase through conversation and reading. But it remains a borrowed memory, not my own. (Halbwachs, 1980:51)

He subsequently problematises 'historical memory' by suggesting that its constituent terms are opposed, in so far as history begins where memory stops (ibid.:78). This formulation recalls Benedict Anderson's dictum that whenever the identity of a person or a nation cannot be remembered it must be narrated, because 'forgetting . . . engenders the need for a narrative of identity' (Anderson, 1991:204, 205).

As Paula Hamilton reminds us, however, it is unwise to assume a simple opposition or rupture between history and memory, since on the contrary they 'nourish' each other (P. Hamilton, 1994:11–13). *red roses* certainly demonstrates the interweaving of memory and history. History, according to Halbwachs, is comprised of that which we cannot remember. The narrator of *red roses* tells us on a number of occasions that she is returning to her mother's time, which is not her own time, and is beyond memory: 'i am returning to a former time in history books they are telling her stories and mine i'm never just here at the right time . . . I am buying old clothes and used clothes to return to a former time. I want to buy my time back. I am getting her time' (Walwicz, 1992a:93, 52). She is recreating the historical events and people in Europe during World War II; although they do not exist as personal memory, they are part of the story of her mother's life and the genealogy of her own ethnicity. Hence she relies on collage as a method of reconstituting this history. As Walter Benjamin understood, while quotations revive historical events, they nevertheless signify that the events they record have passed out of living memory (Carter, 1992:187).

This is why fantasies of origin (and no origin) are scattered through the text of *red roses*. In the first few pages the narrator seeks out her 'certificate of birth' and imagines being an orphan, a child of the new world whose European/old world parents are dead (Walwicz, 1992a:3, 15, 16). This is followed by a number of scenarios in which she invents different parents: 'i was a daughter of barons they left me on her doorstep i was born an egyptian princess'; 'my father was an admiral an owner of hotels she was a opera singer'; 'my parents were french they were fashionable people farming'; 'my parents were nobles in england i was sent to boarding school' (ibid.:16, 18, 19, 37). These fantasies serve to foreground both the dilemma of an autobiographer who cannot remember, and the construction of history in the new world. In personal as in national histories, fiction and invention take over where memory ends.

In the absence of memory, the narrator feels she must fabricate a history; in a self-reflexive text like *red roses*, this creates a heightened awareness (and indeed a celebration of) the role of fiction in creating histories. The text is characterised by an interest in revisiting and rereading the past with postmodern irony. The shift to a flexible and labile definition of origins and ethnicity is not discernible in 'Poland', which is marked by a narrative resistance to 'making things up': 'they ask me where I come from. I say I come from here and here. This is where I am. Here. I don't remember Poland . . . I don't want to tell stories. I don't want to make things up' (Walwicz, 1982:37). The inventive and playful narrator of *red roses*, by contrast, declares she is 'making it all up' (Walwicz, 1992a:95). As she goes on to explain: 'i wanted to make a definitive statements then the defining but there's no such thing now writing is only a game then this is not me or mine and it is not her entirely' (ibid.:184). In the construction of the mother and her history, the narrator admits to 'making up', 'stealing', 'dreaming' and 'inventing' it all (ibid.:32, 49, 120, 128). This begs the question as to whose life story she is creating. The narrator's self-description as 'a beast underground' which has 'come up after thirty five years of being hid' (ibid.:11) may be interpreted (like the later statement that she is writing 'a diary of travels') as an invitation to read *red roses* as autobiography. Comments made by Walwicz in interviews and articles—such as her remark that when writing she 'reconstructs [her] world, through the record of [her] personal experience' (Walwicz, n.d.[a]:14)—would appear to confirm this view. However, she warns us that we cannot reconstruct an autobiographical subject from the use of autobiographical material in her writing. 'The autobiographical aspect has been dismantled right from the start', she declares. 'It is writing which uses autobiography, rather than actually writing autobiography. The persona that develops in the writing is fictitious' (Walwicz, 1992b:829).

In fact, the narrator of *red roses* claims that she is writing the biography of a mother, and that the life stories of mother and daughter merge in 'history': 'i am part of this history in a darkly place of hers' (Walwicz, 1992a:79, 125). In her diasporic shift from the old world to the new, the narrator discards the burdensome history of the former in order to reinvent herself: 'i wanted to invent myself and make myself apart and to be what i wanted i was overburdened with all that history of the town i wanted to be done with all that i wanted to begin just today' (ibid.:176). But the reinvention of herself involves (re)inventing history. In this sense her project is neither autobiographical nor based solely on memory. An awareness of the absence (or at least the disordering and forgetting) of origins leads the writer into fiction and theatre for the purpose of constructing a diasporic history. In fact, as a work in progress, *red roses* was referred to as a novel (Jacobson, 1990:153; Walwicz, 1989b:70; Walwicz, n.d.[b]:19). Fiction is a self-reflexive and playful strategy, a means of reinventing ethnicity and gender. As Fischer (1986) suggests, ethnicity is oriented not just to the past but also to the future. Although memory is the main mode of reinventing ethnicity, forgetting is unavoidable, and in fact necessary in order to move into the future. Where memory stops, fiction steps in. In *red roses*, travel is the metaphor for the fictionality of diasporic worlds.

Geographic separation from the country of origin makes travel back to the country of origin an important mode of rediscovery and reinvention. Like catharsis, travel is a magical process: one returns 'a different person' (Walwicz, 1992a:211). In fact, travel is synonymous with writing in *red roses*, and both are personified in the figure of the magician, who 'travels and travels and does tricks by writing it down' (ibid.:186). The narrator deals in 'flying words', and like the magician she travels 'to do secret rites' (ibid.:117, 30). The figuring of writing as travel, and the process of making meaning as a journey, has been explored by other writers. Brian Castro similarly describes writing as 'a migratory process', the words being 'birds of passage which wing from the subliminal to the page, leaving their signs for the reader' (Castro, 1992:8). According to Iain Chambers, 'to write is . . . to travel'. 'Characterised by movement: the passage of words, the caravan of thought, the flux of the imaginary, the slippage of metaphor', writing 'opens up a space that invites movement, migration, a journey' (I. Chambers, 1994:10). Such images evoke the body. Writing, like travel, is seen as alchemical and magical in *red roses* because it engenders trans-action and change. These processes imply both the performativity of the body and the theatricality of gender and ethnic 'roles'.

Performativity and theatricality are intensified by the return to sites of 'origin', where the interplay of past with present worlds high-lights the fictionality and mutability of ethnicity and gender. The immigrant, that epitome of mutability, is indeed a 'magician of the self' (van Herk, 1991:174).

The traveller has several guises, each for a different role. If she travels back to her homeland as a returning diasporic, she cannot avoid doing so as a tourist. In reconstructing her family history she becomes a tourist in her own past. The cities she returns to are now for her museums (Walwicz, 1992a:165). Even her sense of a homeland is shaped by a touristic desire to claim the other as her own: 'i'm homesick for where i haven't been' (Walwicz, 1989a:72). As a tourist she is reminded that her rereading of history is necessarily fictitious, in so far as tourism (like theatre and film) constructs 'a real and unreal place' (Walwicz, 1992a:176). If the Europe to which the diasporic pilgrim returns is now a museum, her own project of keeping a 'diary of travels' is inevitably archival. Although in our forgetful postmodern age we no longer live within memory, our sensibility remains essentially historical. We therefore construct what Pierre Nora calls *lieux de mémoire* ('sites of memory'). Archives, museums, monuments, festivals and testimonies anchor remnants of memory to sites where a sense of historical continuity persists. *Lieux de mémoire* mark the end of a tradition of memory now reconstituted under the gaze of history. Traditional ('real') memory comprises unstudied gestures, habits, unspoken traditions and the body's inherent self-knowledge; it is social, collective and spontaneous. Modern memory, on the other hand, has been transformed by its passage through history, and is psychological, individual and deliberative. *Lieux de mémoire* make their appearance by 'producing, manifesting, establishing, construct-ing, decreeing, and maintaining by artifice and by will a society deeply absorbed in its own transformation and renewal' (Nora, 1989:12). In our epoch the quest for memory is the search for one's history. Nora describes history as the self-knowledge that enables society to establish continuities with its past. Memory's new vocation, however, is to record. As traditional memory disappears, we feel obliged to collect remains and testimonies. Modern memory is consequently archival, and relies on the materiality of the trace.

Thus memory is transformed into history: or as Nora puts it, memory 'dictates while history writes' (ibid.:21). In the collage-like textuality of *red roses* we can see those traces that characterise 'the realm of history'. The artefact or archive of personal history is assembled through the materiality of language, which makes visible (in fragments and scraps of quotations) the scattered traces of traditional memory.

In the context of *lieux de mémoire*, the personal archival history documented and constructed in *red roses* exemplifies that 'psychologization of contemporary memory' which, in Nora's words, entails a 'completely new economy of the identity of the self, the mechanics of memory and the relevance of the past' (ibid.:15). The anxiety displayed in *red roses* to constitute or 'stick together' a history indicates the need to create a sense of continuity between the Europe of the past and the diasporic's present in the new world—to create, in short, a history of diaspora. Because memory has become individualised and 'private' in our age, Walwicz's narrative is personalised rather than collective. While it could be read as articulating experiences common to immigrants, there is a sense in which it is specific and particular. As merely one among many heterogeneous narratives of migration, it is located in its own historical specificities.

As Nora points out, archives can be transformed into *lieux de mémoire* if they are invested with a symbolic aura. The 'museumisation' of national origin, and the transformation of the archive of the self into literature (and specifically, in the Australian context, into 'migrant' or 'multicultural' literature), invest the text with just such an aura. In entering the canon of Australian literature, *red roses* becomes a *lieu de mémoire*.

## Ania Walwicz and Australian literature

If the memorial and archival consciousness of *red roses* constructs a personal history, so too does Walwicz's commentary on the relation of her own writing to Australian literature. Setting up an opposition between 'Australian' and 'European' literature, she identifies with the 'historical progression' of European modernism, and specifically with the traditions of Fauvism, Dadaism, Surrealism and Expressionism (Walwicz, n.d.[b]:10). 'The origins of my work all lead to European literature', she told Jenny Digby (Walwicz, 1992b:834): 'I consider my European identity to go before anything else, because that goes back to my childhood' (Walwicz, n.d.[b]:10). In her interview with Digby she quotes from her prose piece 'europe' to emphasise this point: 'i'm Europe' (ibid.). She privileges her European origins above her identity and experience as an immigrant: 'that heritage is more important to me than the migrant experience which just dealt with denial of my cultural heritage, denial of myself for a certain period of time' (ibid.:11). Described here as a 'denial', migration is 'a destructive, demeaning experience' (ibid.).

It is possible to trace a narrative of progression in Walwicz's *oeuvre* from the painful memory of the past recorded in *writing* (1982) to an affirmation of her European heritage in *red roses* (1992). In *writing*, the passage of migration is characterised by tropes of transfiguration, discovery and newness on the one hand, and of loss and estrangement on the other. As Sue Gillet has pointed out, the emphatic insistence in *writing* on newness, arrival, beginning and birth is figured as change and escape rather than a retrieval of or return to origins (Gillet, 1991:240). The past is represented as a place where the speaker is constrained, repressed and sick (ibid.). In 'Poland' (first published in 1982), the homeland left by the narrator is depicted not nostalgically but as an absence and unbridgeable distance (ibid.:251). This does not imply a simple opposition between a good new country and a bad old one, since migration is represented as a demeaning and belittling experience in 'Australia' (1981), 'no speak' (1982, published in *writing*), 'wogs' (1987) and 'vampire' (1988). It is significant that in the two earlier pieces Walwicz assumes the persona of the migrant in order to focus on experiences of anger and disempowerment, whereas the narrative persona in the two later pieces is that of an Anglo-Saxon 'ocker' Aussie, a framing effect which invites us to read them parodically.

Walwicz's second book, *boat* (1989), tends to shift away from the experience of migration and to focus on origins and heritage. It is as if the pressure to assimilate has required at least a temporary amnesia or repression of the past. That process is reversed by the time *boat* appears, for in 'europe' (first published in 1985) the speaker says: 'they took my europe away . . . but i bounce back . . . i'm europe again' (Walwicz, 1989a:71). This focus on Europe intensifies in her third book, *red roses*, with its motifs of travel, and return, and the rewriting and excavation of history. Here Europe is called into being through its absence: it is both a condition and a product of the narrator's exile. As Vijay Mishra (1994) points out, it is diasporas that create homelands. Or as Karen Fog Olwig puts it, 'home is where you leave it' (Olwig, 1993:137).

Walwicz contrasts her European heritage and her interest in the avant-garde with an Australian literature characterised by social realism and a sense of place. She considers that in form and setting her work has little in common with Australian literature: 'I am a living reaction to Australian literature' (Walwicz, 1992b:823). She considers that because of her interest in avant-garde writing she occupies 'a vulnerable place within the Australian literary set-up where there is no avant-garde whatsoever' (ibid.:834). She recognises, however, that her literary success has made her in fact 'part of Australian literature' (ibid.:835).

In her article on Walwicz, Lisa Jacobson traces this opposition between avant-garde or marginalised writing and the canon of Australian literature. She effects a reconciliation of sorts by suggesting that Walwicz, although now canonised, 'eschews a conventional entrance into the canon' by 'strategically avoiding any forms of phallocentric . . . or . . . "Anglocentric" assimilation'. Despite this recognition of gender and ethnic differences, Jacobson goes on to suggest that Walwicz's 'successful acceptance into Australian literature [is] as an Australian writer rather than a female or migrant writer' (Jacobson, 1990:158).

Many non-Anglo-Celtic writers shun the ghettoisation implied by the label 'multicultural', and aspire to be incorporated into the mainstream of Australian literature (see, for example, Lewitt, 1992; Safransky, 1992). The formation of a constituency of 'multicultural' and 'migrant' writers may well have been strategically necessary in Australia in the 1970s and 1980s as a resistance to assimilation. But the continuing separatism of this constituency in the 1990s has a marginalising rather than an interventionary effect. Perhaps we should take our cue from Canadian practice, and redefine the centre instead of merely confirming the margins. As Sneja Gunew suggests, we should talk about 'ethnicity in literature' rather than ethnic literatures (Gunew, 1993:453). Or to put it another way, 'multiculturalism will only function as a useful expression of difference when it is seen as including Anglo-Celts' (Gunew, 1990a:115).

Certainly Walwicz has indicated her reluctance to be classified as an 'ethnic', 'multicultural' or 'migrant' writer. Despite her radicalism in matters of literary form, she insists that she does not represent 'radical ideology', and she aims to be published by mainstream publishing (Walwicz, 1992b:835). Her claim that 'innovative writing doesn't exist as a category yet' in Australian literature (Walwicz, n.d.[b]:20) is belied by her success. Perhaps it has been easier for such texts to enter the canon as examples of 'migrant' or 'multicultural' writing, where formal experimentation is legitimised by cultural difference. Walwicz's *oeuvre* thus constitutes a moment of globalisation in Australian literature. Writing in her dual capacity as an immigrant in Australia who wants to travel to the homeland ('i want the coming back': Walwicz, 1991:194), Walwicz articulates the diasporic consciousness of being split between 'where you're from' and 'where you're at' (Ang, 1993; Gilroy, 1991). Her own formal and generic affiliation with the European avant-garde demonstrates that writing is not necessarily contained by national borders.

Sneja Gunew has drawn attention to the ways in which 'migrant' writing has been read in Australia as unmediated experience. Because 'migrant' writers are considered informants, their work is treated as sociology or history rather than as literature framed by conventions of fiction (Gunew, 1990a:113). First-person narratives are often read as confessions: the more disordered the language, the more authentic it supposedly sounds. They tend to be valued according to their linguistic 'naivety' and 'incompetence', which are taken to indicate the degree to which narrators and authors have been assimilated or naturalised (Gunew, 1986:65–6). Yet as Gillian Bottomley points out, the ability to delineate a private sphere is an attribute of social power (Bottomley, 1992:156). To read first-person narratives not as oral history but fiction certainly increases the cultural capital of a writer like Walwicz, whose project is not invested with the political agenda of Aboriginal women's autobiographical narratives, for example, which claim a different private sphere and therefore rewrite history from quite a different point of view. The private sphere from which Walwicz 'writes back' takes its bearings from the European avant-garde, and is situated in opposition to the Australian social realist canon. Walwicz claims the power to reinvent herself. In exposing the fictionality of such genres as autobiography and biography, she critiques those nationalistic readings of 'migrant' writing that treat it as ethnography.

# 5

# Formations of Nationalism: Arthur Yap and Philip Jeyaretnam

The travel motifs in Ania Walwicz's *red roses* clearly figure migrancy rather than national situatedness or being firmly situated by the national culture. If cosmopolitanism can be defined as '"belonging" to parts of the world other than one's nation' (Robbins, 1992:173), then the collage-like textuality of *red roses* articulates a global or cosmopolitan identity. As an intertextual medium, collage embodies the instability and contingent nature of meaning and representation, and therefore evokes dislocation and discontinuity. Ethnicity and gender are treated in *red roses* as performative and provisional rather than essentialist or fixed. Walwicz's text thus creates the discursive conditions for an alternative to originary, nativist or ethnicist discourses of nationalist multiculturalism. In effect it parodies multiculturalism's project of institutionalising, or officially recording, memory and museumising ethnicity.

James Clifford (1992) argues that contemporary culture is characterised as much by travel as by dwelling and residence. This description is particularly relevant to the immigrant and multiracial societies of Singapore and Australia. Clifford calls for new maps of such societies, which he describes as 'borderland culture areas, populated by strong, diasporic ethnicities unevenly assimilated to dominant nation states' (Clifford, 1992:110). In composing these new maps, he suggests, we need 'to take travel knowledges seriously' (ibid.:105).

I would like to consider here the issue of nationalism in relation to Singaporean literature, and to investigate how we might map Singaporean nationalism in ways which accommodate the everyday urban life of the multiracial (the preferred term in Singapore), cosmopolitan and diasporic population of Singapore. Instead of describing Singaporean culture in terms of travel and migrancy, I would like to look at the motifs of what Clifford calls 'dwelling and residence', and specifically at how the city—that epitome of Singaporean experience—is constructed in Singaporean literature. I want to argue that the city is a zone of indeterminacy where two or more cultural referential codes cohabit, and where identities are consequently 'in the making' or 'in process'. For the city is a site of provisional representations where, to repeat Clifford's words, 'diasporic ethnicities [are] unevenly assimilated to dominant nation states'. In mapping the social space of the city I want to focus upon descriptions of everyday life in the writings of two Singaporeans: the short-story writer and novelist, Philip Jeyaretnam, and the poet Arthur Yap.

Geoffrey Benjamin has called Singapore 'one of the most thoroughly colonized societies known to history' (Benjamin, 1976:131). Its movement towards independence in the 1950s and early 1960s, and its subsequent transformation into a highly industrialised and multiracial republic, have relied heavily on the discourse of nationalism as fashioned on two principal sites: literature and the university. On the eve of independence in 1965, the Singaporean Prime Minister, Lee Kuan Yew, spoke of the need to 'transform a colonial institution [the university] . . . into a centre of higher learning where our youths are trained and imbued and inspired with the ideals of building our new nation' (Lee Kuan Yew, 1964:18). Two decades later, the Head of the Department of English and Dean of the Faculty of Arts at the National University of Singapore, Professor Edwin Thumboo, stated that 'academic disciplines, including ours . . . cannot function detached from the processes of nation-building' (Thumboo, 1985:53).

Singaporean nationalism, like that of many post-colonial countries, functions primarily as a mechanism for planning and propaganda. Social engineering has long been a vigorous force in the cultural development of Singapore, which Teh Cheang Wan (a former Minister for National Development) described as 'one of the most planning-conscious countries in the world' (Teh, 1979:24). One of the most pressing and persuasive demands on behalf of nationalism in Singapore has been for a national literary tradition. Ever since the inception of the University of Malaya in 1949, the discourse of literary criticism has been vocal in its demand for first a Malayan and then a Singaporean literature (Brewster, 1989; forthcoming). Literary texts are read inevitably in the context of literary criticism. In Singapore, literary criticism has been part of the discourse of a nationalism that first articulated the country's emergence from colonialism, and later its rapid economic development and commitment to modernisation.

## Everyday life and the city

'Everyday life' is by no means a self-evident phenomenon in social analysis. Agnes Heller describes it as 'the foundation of all human knowledge, action, of all types of rationality' and of all social institutions (Heller, 1985:81, 86). Patrick Wright (quoting Kosik) describes everyday life as 'above all the organising of people's individual lives into every day: the replicability of their life functions is fixed in the replicability of every day' (Wright, 1985:6). Everyday life, Wright adds, is

> the historically conditioned framework in which the imperatives of natural sustenance (eating, sleeping . . .) come to be socially determined: it is in the intersubjectivity of everyday life that human self-reproduction is welded to the wider process of social reproduction . . . At the heart of everyday life, therefore, is the interdependency of person and society. (ibid.:6–7)

Basing his own analysis on Heller's work, Wright sees everyday life as reflecting a 'vernacular and informal sense of history' (ibid.:5).

In his essay on 'The Culture of Nations' (1983), Raymond Williams notes how the 'imagined community' of the nation derives from local bonding in the smallest social units, such as families, villages and towns, and even particular streets or parts of a town. I would like to suggest that this 'everyday' sense of the historical and of 'local bonding' can be the basis of a discourse of nationalism. When nationalism becomes institutionalised, however, it loses its links with popular and grass-roots notions of the 'imagined community'. Official uses of nationalistic rhetoric tend to deny the complexity of everyday life. In Edward Said's words: 'the truth of lived communal (or personal) experience has often been totally sublimated in official narratives, institutions and ideologies' (Said, 1987:158).

Philip Jeyaretnam's first book, *First Loves* (1987), a collection of stories, was a Singaporean best-seller; he has published two novels since then, *Raffles Place Ragtime* (1989) and *Abraham's Promise* (1995). I would like to look briefly at a story from *First Loves*, and specifically at its representation of two formations of everyday (city) life, where images of dwelling and residence construct notions of local bonding. One of the characters of *First Loves*, Ah Leong, speculates about the social bonding that might occur 'horizontally' between high-rise apartments:

> He felt a special affinity for all those who dwelt on the tenth floor. They ought to form a community, bound together by their horizontal ties. He wondered about the blocks on higher ground. Should their tenth floors form part of his community? Should his community be one of height relative to the ground? Or height relative to sea level? If it was height relative to sea level then other floors in some blocks would gain access to his community. But there could not be many such blocks. Singapore had been flattened for land reclamation, the hills dumped in the sea. Perhaps this flattening had helped create horizontal communities, perhaps the rubbing out of individual neighbourhoods by bulldozers and concrete mixers brought closer the higher ideal of national unity, unity born of sharing the same level of airspace? (Jeyaretnam, 1987:8)

Given that a large percentage of Singapore's population lives in high-rise apartments, the experience of high-rise living is obviously 'national' in the sense that it typifies an 'imagined community' whose members, to quote Benedict Anderson again, 'will never know most of their fellow-members, meet them, or even hear of them, yet in the minds of each lives the image of their communion' (Anderson, 1991:6). Jeyaretnam's playful figuring of lived experience and local bonding in the image of horizontal communities literally constructs everyday urban life in Singapore in a way that subverts official images of nationalism.

Another site in Jeyaretnam's fiction of the local bonding of everyday urban life is the formation of ethnicity in the minority family. In Australian Aboriginal women's autobiographical narratives, the family is a site of Aboriginal people's resistance to assimilation. The family plays a similar role in other minority groups, such as Indians in Singapore, whose ethnicity is a site for the maintenance of difference. 'Minority individuals are always treated and forced to experience themselves generically', write JanMohamed and Lloyd (1987:10). In the story called 'A New Eye' the Indian narrator, Rajiv, comes into conflict with his parents on account of his Chinese girlfriend. He describes his parents as people who

> live as if under siege. They have ceded control over public life, over political decisions, to others, to Chinese people. We are outsiders they say. Never rock the boat or we will be the ones thrown off. So respect the will of the majority. And, to compensate for this concession, they have raised ramparts to shelter behind. Their powerlessness beyond the gates has made them all the more defiant at home. We must maintain our identity, our solidarity. Marry within our people, son. (Jeyaretnam, 1987:41–2)

In response to their powerlessness, Rajiv's parents assert their ethnic and racial difference. Ethnicity is thus determined as much by social positioning as by innate characteristics. Love, desire and marriage are for minority groups far from merely 'private' or domestic concerns; they become political issues that are played out in the everyday life of the family. Rajiv, for example, defects from his parents' views: 'I cannot accept . . . their straightjacket [sic]' (ibid.:46), he says, and continues his relationship with his Chinese girlfriend. Ethnicity, as Rajiv sees it, is not fixed and essentialist but continually in process. It is located not so much in the past as in the indeterminacy of the present, and it is future-oriented. Ethnicity is not something simply passed on from generation to generation, to be taught and learned (Fischer, 1986:195). On the contrary, it is performative, provisional and dynamic, and each generation reinvents and renegotiates it.

This view of ethnicity and culture as continuing processes militates against the stereotyping of race and ethnicity in official statements about culture, multiracialism and nationalism. In his depiction of the family and the formation of ethnicity, Jeyaretnam gives voice to what Clifford describes as 'diasporic ethnicities . . . unevenly assimilated into the dominant nation states' (Clifford, 1992:110). And in this alternative narrative of 'uneven assimilation' we can see the emergence of what Homi Bhabha describes as 'national, anti-nationalist, histories of the "people"' (Bhabha, 1988:22). Jeyaretnam's short stories suggest ways of mapping the multiracial population of Singapore without foreclosing on different formations of ethnicity, that is, without fixing ethnicity in stereotypical and essentialist terms.

Arthur Yap is a prize-winning poet who has published four books of poetry that articulate a nationalism working at a popular and local level. The opposition of private versus public, which was common in Singaporean literary criticism of the 1960s and 1970s, has been invoked in discussions of Yap's poetry. There it was used to emphasise the (public) responsibilities of the poet in the project of nation building. It is invoked by Ee Tiang Hong in his Foreword to *commonplace* (1977), Yap's second book. Disputing the notion that the poet has a public duty to be a mouthpiece of nationalism, Ee legitimises those 'private' poets who have 'not felt it necessary to explain their society'. The problem with this reversal is that it leaves intact the opposition of public to private. Yap's poetry, however, in its interest in 'commonplace' everyday life, demonstrates that this opposition is fictional. This is because so-called public and private domains are constantly being mediated by citizens in the course of their everyday lives.

In 'dramatis personae'—a poem from his third book, *down the line* (1980)—Yap explores the theatre of everyday life as it is lived in three public places: the park, the beach and the pond. Repetition is emphasised, and especially in the ritualistic leisure activities that take place 'day after day' in these public places. It is not a question here of private individuals against public places. Instead, people are seen as 'acting out' their everyday lives (the title 'dramatis personae' foregrounds the notion of performance) in both private and public places. In the theatre of everyday life we observe the interdependency of person and society. These are poems about being citizens. There is a sense of pleasure in the actions of the dramatis personae—pleasure in the repetition (or, in Kosik's words, 'replicability') and ritual of everyday life. The imagery of these poems also conveys a sense of poignancy at the loss of certain small freedoms: the flowers in the park are not to be picked, because 'they are for the public'; the land-crabs—'webbed', 'sewn' and 'trapped' by their concrete environment—are a telling metaphor; and the little boys' carefree play among the weeds is contrasted with 'the lesson/on fish & waterlife & diagrams' that they must endure elsewhere. The mood of 'dramatis personae' is one of both renewal (through pleasure and organised leisure) and resignation to the repetitiveness of the ritual.

A second poem, 'down the line', also takes place in the theatre of public space, but this time in the city. The city state, for all its visual magnificence, is a place of work. The notion of everyday labour is evoked once again in the image of land-crabs, labouring on the beach where they

> lay at the water's edge a library of margins.
> page by page, it prefabricates the day's
> ins & outs but, like pure callisthenics,
> seem never quite enough. (Yap, 1980:10)

The repetition of daily work is described here as 'pure callisthenics', and the nation is seen as the site of discipline. The poem contains a pointed critique of the discourse of social engineering, the propaganda of official nationalism: 'what everyone will tell you is what everyone/wants to hear, has been told'; 'credulity is a bigger commodity than credibility'.

Another poem that depicts everyday life is 'shipwreck', whose titular image of the Singapore skyline is a metaphor for the daily city-life of the nation:

> a shipwreck is a tall shore of humanity.
> with an island background, it had been composed
> on sand, dry inland, crafted by hand.

it can be seen in the city, daily,
neatly. (ibid.:3)

A play on the title produces a new image:

sheepwreck: (as i imagine) in animate collision,
each impact cushioned. do i say to you:
let us not pull the wool over each other's eyes
(& other civilities)?

The image of people 'in animate collision,/each impact cushioned'
is a brilliant description of their everyday interactions, determined
as they are by the ever pervasive propaganda of nationalism.

The sense of history recorded in these poems is what Patrick
Wright (1980) would call 'vernacular' and 'informal'. Each conveys
a clear sense that Singaporean people have a national history, and
that their nation is the product of a great deal of labour, effort,
discipline and sacrifice. Yap, I argue, is a poet of the quotidian,
who accepts the banal and the mundane for their intrinsic value in
the repetitions of everyday life. They are not mystified or transformed into myth in a way represented by the titles of Edwin
Thumboo's collections of poetry, *Gods Can Die* (1977) and *Ulysses
by the Merlion* (1979). Nor are they universalised in the rhetoric of
official nationalism, or passed over in preference to either the
'auratic' objects (i.e. those invested with the aura) of high-cultural
tourism (such as the merlion) or the lyrical and confessional world
of the individualised bourgeois ego. And yet, in rendering the
banality and mundanity of everyday life, Yap tells us something
important about the formation of what the political theorist Antonio
Gramsci calls 'the national popular'. For as Heller argues, the banality
and the mundanity of everyday life constitute the 'foundation of all
human knowledge' (Heller, 1985:81).

In 'down the line' Yap critiques the totalising discourse of official
nationalism. He discovers instead a kind of grass-roots nationalism,
an informal bonding which takes place at the local level. The
informal history of a people and a nation is based on memory, and
memory is local before it can be national. Anthony D. Smith observes
that myth and memory lie at the heart of nationalism, and that
'there can be no identity without memory' (Smith, 1986:2). Memory

is not simply a national or collective phenomenon; its roots are formed in individuals in the process of everyday life.

If these poems epitomise citizenship, they also bear traces of a nostalgia which decreases in intensity after the publication of Yap's first two volumes, although it is still evident in his last two. Nostalgia is not rebellion, for these citizens accept their lot, but it nevertheless subverts official constructions of history. Memory and history are processes by which we negotiate the relation of past to present in our everyday lives. To engage actively with the past in the present is to live in and with a sense of loss. The official nationalism of a modernising nation necessarily plays down the price paid for progress. But this price lives on in the memory of its citizens, and is evident in the sense of resignation, acceptance and endurance that is characteristic of Yap's poetry.

Nationalism has been scrutinised by theorists from both developing and developed nations. Among those sceptical of nationalism is South American Jean Franco. She describes how Latin American nation states were 'vehicles for (often enforced) capitalist modernisation . . . [which] occurred for the most part without grass-roots participation or any form of democratic debate and was often vehiculated by autocratic or populist/authoritarian regimes' (Franco, 1989:205). She criticises nationalism for both 'its failure to provide systems of meaning and belief' and its inability to mediate 'the continent's uneasy and unfinished relationship with modernity' (ibid.:208, 211). She concludes that the nation 'is no longer the inevitable framework for either cultural or political projects' (ibid.:204).

Raymond Williams echoes this pessimism. For him the nation is an obsolescent category that is at once 'too large and too small for the range of real social purposes': it is too large 'to develop full social identities in their real diversity', and too small to survive the trading and monetary necessities of the global context (Williams, 1983:197). Concluding that nations 'are political forms that now limit, subordinate and destroy people', he urges us 'to begin again with people and build new political forms' (ibid.:199). In spite of critiques by theorists like Franco and Williams, however, there may still be a place for alternative nationalisms that arise from grass-roots concerns. Examples are to be found in Carolyn Cooper's work on Jamaican reggae (1993) and in the opposition by Aboriginal people to multinational mining industries in Australia. Modernity and capitalism have led to the disenchantment of the world. But as Patrick Wright points out, the craving for a re-enchantment of the world will not 'find satisfaction in the unitary and exclusive image of the imperial nation' (Wright, 1985:26). If so, then perhaps a popular nationalism would enable such a re-enchantment.

# 6

# Neo-nationalism and Post-coloniality: Bharati Mukherjee

Like Ania Walwicz, Bharati Mukherjee articulates the experience of migration and relocation. Unlike Walwicz, however, she emigrated to a culture that had imperialist links with the country of her birth, India. Her interpellation into her 'host' country is therefore conditioned by post-coloniality. Mukherjee lived first in Canada, where she was a citizen from 1966–80, after which she emigrated to the USA. Canada, like Australia, had a strict Immigration Act (1923); although it was repealed in 1947, Asian entry was minimal until the relaxation of immigration laws in the 1960s (Thorpe, 1991:5). The USA has also had high rates of Asian immigration since the 1960s; in 1984 Asians made up 44 per cent of immigrants, and the Asian population was estimated to have grown by 84 per cent in the 1980s (Chua, 1992:51). Certainly in the 1980s the immigrant population was much higher in Australia (21.6 per cent) than either Canada (15.2 per cent) or the USA (4.7 per cent) (Pettman, 1992b:35). Ironically, however, Mukherjee's literary success occurred at a time when the theme of immigration into the new world was (re)enshrined in the myth of what it is to be American, and on a scale not yet seen in Australia. In this chapter I examine how Mukherjee's romance of immigration has facilitated a reinvention of American nationalism, and how the post-coloniality that enables her transnational mobility is disavowed in the process.

Generally speaking, discussions of 'migrant' or 'multicultural' writing in Australia foreground its counter-discursivity and the ways in which it interrogates the literary canon. As a result, 'ethnicity' is set in opposition to official nationalism, as Sneja Gunew suggests:

In its traditional usage, culture is associated with the nation state; but because most such entities are now increasingly aware of their multicultural mix, the concept of cultural minorities or ethnicities is useful in undermining a centrist construction of culture as a privileged discourse concerned with the definition of core values . . . The recognition of 'ethnicity' as a category of difference thus serves as safeguard against the development of imperialisms or 'nationalisms'. (Gunew, 1990b:24–5)

In contrast to this 'Australian' line of argument, Mukherjee's discourse on migrants in the USA positions them not on the margins of contemporary American culture but as exemplars of a hegemonic nationalism. Far from being oppositional to mainstream America, migrants represent the voice of 'the new America' (Mukherjee, 1989:73) and thus, I argue, enunciate a neo-nationalism. Mukherjee's own literary success places her firmly within the American literary canon. It indicates the receptivity of certain constituencies to the reinvention and revitalisation of American nationalism.

Mukherjee's discourse of nationalism is articulated in both her fiction and her autobiographical writings. Her first three novels and two collections of stories create narratives of the entry into American culture of immigrants from a variety of ethnic back-grounds, for the most part Indian. She also constructs a personal mythology of immigration and 'assimilation' which is deployed in numerous autobiographical and quasi-autobiographical writings: these take the generic form of non-fiction, interviews, essays and articles (the latter often comprise readings of her own fiction). In her non-fictional writing (and specifically in interviews and arti-cles) Mukherjee endorses the notion of 'assimilation', contrasting American assimilationist policy with what she sees as the less successful Canadian 'mosaic' policy of multiculturalism (Blaise and Mukherjee, 1987, quoted in Goodwin, 1989:412). Her endorsement of American nationalism is paralleled by the canonisation of her fiction. In 1988 her second collection of stories, *The Middleman and Other Stories*, won the National Book Critics Circle Award, which 'is given by the organisation of 485 professional book editors and critics from across the country and carries more clout in literary circles . . . than the National Book Awards [sponsored by the publishing industry] or the Pulitzer Prize' (Patel, 1989:72). Since then she has had front-page reviews in the *New York Times Book Review*, has published high-profile articles in such magazines as *Harper's Bazaar*, and has been invited to literary festivals in Canada, New Zealand and Australia.

Both Mukherjee's fiction and her attitude to immigration and nationalism follow the trajectory of her own migrations. Her 'early' work comprises a couple of novels, *The Tiger's Daughter* (1972) and *Wife* (1975); the three Canadian pieces in her first short-story collection, *Darkness* (1985), namely 'The World According to Hsü', 'Isolated Incidents' and 'Tamurlane'; and, from *The Middleman and Other Stories* (1988), 'The Management of Grief'. These are separated from her later work by a space of ten years (1975–85), during which time she emigrated from Canada to the USA. With the exception of *The Tiger's Daughter* and a number of stories, her early work is set in Canada and generally articulates pessimism, anger and a sense of homelessness. In 'The World According to Hsü', for example, Ratna Clayton—a woman married to a Canadian academic and bitter about Canadian racism—holidays among a hotch-potch of tourists on a island off the coast of Africa, and muses that 'no matter where she lived, she would never feel so at home again' (Mukherjee, 1986:56).

*Wife*, in its depiction of the central character's alienation and depression, also articulates a bleak vision of an immigrant woman's failure to 'assimilate' into western culture. Although the novel is set in New York city, Mukherjee has revealed that in fact it reflects her own life in Toronto (Mukherjee, 1981:39; Goodwin, 1989:411). *Wife* and the later novel *Jasmine* (which articulates what I have called neo-nationalism) are in this respect antithetical to one another. For whereas Dimple (the protagonist of *Wife*) is timid and passive, Jasmine is courageous and active. As the following episode suggests, Dimple does not make Jasmine's successful transition into American culture:

Ina doodled on the margin of a leaflet until there was a woman with her sari wrapped around her like a shroud on one side and another woman in a bikini with a pert bosom on the other. 'That's me,' she said, with a shallow laugh. 'Before and After. The great moral and physical change, and all that.'

'I'm always a Before,' Dimple said. 'I guess I've never been an After.' (Mukherjee, 1987b:95)

By distinguishing sharply between her Canadian and American phases, Mukherjee quite consciously shapes and prescribes a reading position for her fiction. 'By the time I came to write *The Middleman*', she says, 'I was exhilarated, my vision was more optimistic' (Mukherjee, 1990d:28). She characterises the collection as her 'tribute to America' (Patel, 1989:72), and describes *Jasmine* in similar terms: 'I want this novel . . . just like the last book of stories [*The Middleman*], to be seen as providing an optimistic vision of America' (Mukherjee, 1990c:221). The heady exuberance of *Jasmine* and Mukherjee's reading of the novel's celebratory nationalism contrast markedly with the disillusionment of *Wife* and the bitterness of her seminal article on racism, 'An Invisible Woman' (1981), with its scathing critique of Canadian racism.

This movement—from Canada to the USA, from pessimism to optimism, from racism and homelessness to a celebration of as-similationist nationalism—is even more significant in terms of Mukherjee's career-path from relative anonymity and lack of recog-nition in Canada (Mukherjee, 1981:39) to award-winning success and canonisation in the USA. As Patel reports, it was with *The Middleman* that Mukherjee 'found her true literary identity—something that she claims coincided with her discovery of herself as an American' (Patel, 1989:72–3).

An earlier starting point is post-colonial India and the 'bi-culturalism' of Mukherjee's first novel, *The Tiger's Daughter*, which explores the post-colonial dilemma of an English-educated and elite expatriate on a return visit to India. The central character, Tara, is something of an outcast in this society because of her 'mleccha' husband, and feels alienated from her friends and their way of life—which are depicted (and exoticised) from an outsider's viewpoint. The narrator mourns the decline of Calcutta in the face of a communist-inspired populist uprising; there is no place in this world for the likes of Tara. The world-weariness and *Angst* of this novel culminates in the violence of rape: Tara is assaulted by an unscrupulous politician, who is in the process of dispossessing the peasants of their land in the name of industrial progress. Needless to say, the novel closes with Tara's passionate statement of attachment to her American husband (who had remained at home in the USA) and her desperate wish to 'get out of Calcutta' (Mukherjee, 1987a:210).

The experience of a post-colonial elite is inevitably 'bicultural', a term Mukherjee herself uses to describe *The Tiger's Daughter* (Mukherjee, 1989:73), and biculturalism is an experience of detachment and irony. She states that in her later writing she rejects the ironical voice that narrates *The Tiger's Daughter*. Such irony— typical of exiled expatriates such as V. S. Naipaul—is 'mordant and self-protective', she says. It 'promised both detachment from, and superiority over, those well-bred postcolonials much like myself, adrift in the New World, wondering if they would ever belong' (Seligman, 1986:38). But ultimately what it promised was not what she wanted.

## The new America

Mukherjee rejects the nostalgia of her early book (as well as the myth of the nomad 'adrift') in order to affirm belonging and to thematise the successful 'conquest' of the new world. In an interview she describes as a 'new pioneer' the immigrant in *The Middleman* (Mukherjee, 1989:73); and she calls the eponymous character of *Jasmine* 'a conqueror, a minor hero' (Healey, 1988:22). In rejecting the experience of expatriation as figured in *The Tiger's Daughter*, she puts in its place the myth of the immigrant. Expatriation, she argues, is 'the great temptation . . . of the ex-colonial . . . writer' (such as Naipaul). Instead she endorses its 'opposite', immigration (Mukherjee, 1988:28). Once again she figures this transformation in geographical terms: in Canada she was a 'psychological expatriate' (ibid.), in the USA an immigrant and a citizen. Not to undergo this conversion from expatriation to immigration is in Mukherjee's eyes evidence of nostalgia, and a refusal to participate in the new world by embracing its citizenship and nationalism. To reject what it offers is to fail as a writer: 'lacking a country, avoiding all the messiness of rebirth as an immigrant, eventually harms even the finest sensibility' (ibid., 1988:28). She numbers Salman Rushdie among those writers who choose 'exile' and dispossession rather than psychological citizenship.

Mukherjee's 'conversion' narrative invests India with the status of the old world figured as repressive. India represents for her 'that kind of Third World hierarchy where your opportunities are closed by caste, gender, or family' (Mukherjee, 1990c:219). For the elite post-colonials of *The Tiger's Daughter*, as well as for Mukherjee herself, India is 'past [its] prime' (Mukherjee, 1981:36), and threatens the existence of that English-educated elite she identifies with: 'the class of women I belonged to . . . has become more or less extinct' (Mukherjee, 1990c:219). She goes on to say that 'the old world no longer excited [her] in ways that the new world did': she found 'the loss of old culture . . . exciting . . . [and] *exhilarating*', and 'was thrilled to have the opportunity to give it up, to assume a new identity' (ibid.:219–20). The process of abandoning the old order is explored most fully in *The Tiger's Daughter* and in her first non-fiction book, *Days and Nights in Calcutta*, which she co-authored with Clark Blaise. The 'conversion', then, rests upon the discarding or abandoning of the old order (Vignisson, 1992–93:160), and the embracing of the new:

> I was [bicultural] when I wrote *The Tiger's Daughter*; now I am no longer so and America is more real to me than India . . . I need to belong. America matters to me. It is not that India failed me—rather America transformed me . . . I realised I was no longer an expatriate but an immigrant—that my life was more here. (Mukherjee, 1989:73)

The new world is figured as a place where anyone can be a success. The immigrants whom Mukherjee writes about 'make their futures in ways that they could not have done in the Old World' (Hancock, 1987:303). They are individuals who need only 'gumption' to make it (Vignisson, 1992–93:168). Mukherjee stresses the 'battler' quality of her characters, and romanticises the struggle of the individual: 'these immigrants are grabby and greedy—and I'm using these words in healthy ways. Larger than life. Eager. In order to be American you have to hustle' (Mukherjee, 1990c:220). Such qualities are further romanticised in her most recent novel, *The Holder of the World* (1993). Its central character—a seventeenth-century American, Hannah—has adventures in India which epitomise those qualities of initiative and 'gumption' that Mukherjee identifies as quintessentially American.

Timothy Brennan includes Mukherjee in a group of what he calls Third World cosmopolitan writers, whom he hails for their 'vision of democracy, freedom, "popularity", "truth"—largely lost or devalued in the metropolis [which is] seen as an arena of disintegration and postmodern decentring' (Brennan, 1989:39). However, this myth of democracy and freedom, which Brennan accurately attributes to Mukherjee, is somewhat eroded by Mukherjee's own admission that she enters the new world already endowed with considerable privilege. Of her departure from India in 1961 as a young woman, for example, she writes: 'great privilege had been conferred upon me . . . I had built-in advantages: primarily those of education, secondarily those of poise and grooming' (Mukherjee, 1981:36). And this privilege is characteristic of many Indians because of the particular nature of their diaspora. As William Safran notes, in the USA the 'Indian diaspora status has not always been associated with political disability or even minority status' (Safran, 1991:88). Gayatri Spivak makes a similar observation about the privileges enjoyed by diasporic Indians of her own generation:

> as the only colored community . . . in the US that did not have a history of oppression on the soil, they were often used in affirmative action employment and admission where blacks, Hispanics, and 'Asian-Americans' (meaning US citizens of Chinese and Japanese extraction) were bypassed. (Spivak, 1989a:278)

The impulse to romanticise occurs in the gap between Mukherjee's own personal history and the social backgrounds of her fictional characters. For although they are not always endowed with the privileges of their author (many are in fact peasants or working class), they inevitably succeed in the new world. Class, racial and ethnic differences are elided in Mukherjee's equation of her own experience with that of immigrants in general. This tendency becomes more marked in the later 'American' phase of her fiction, where her characters are not only Indian but hail from other areas of the globe, such as the Philippines, Iraq, Italy, Afghanistan, Vietnam, the Caribbean and Africa. Clearly, in this phase of her work, Mukherjee no longer feels constrained to speak for or from her own ethnic or class background. Instead she embraces different versions of the 'exotic'. And as her own commentary on her fiction indicates, in doing so she subsumes various immigrant experiences under the stereotype of that tough, hustling, 'grabby and greedy' battler, whom she has also called the 'conqueror', the 'minor hero', the 'new pioneer'.

Mukherjee's romance of immigration—and of a new world of democracy, freedom and unlimited possibility—is figured vividly at the close of *Jasmine*, when Bud's adopted Vietnamese son, Du, leaves his American 'family' to be reunited with his immigrant sister. This event is figured in terms of an Oedipal struggle as Jasmine, the narrator, acknowledges the immigrant's destiny to 'inherit' America. She observes that Du 'was given to us to save and to strengthen; we didn't own him, his leaving was inevitable. Even healthy' (Mukherjee, 1990a:224). His eyes 'glittery with a higher mission', Du 'steps into his future' (ibid.:221, 223). In a parallel allegory, Jasmine leaves the crippled old man in Iowa for a younger man in California: 'I am not choosing between men', she says. 'I am caught between the promise of America and old-world dutiful-ness' (ibid.:240).

I have suggested that Mukherjee's privileged entry into the USA, like that of many Indians, places her in a position different to that of many other immigrants. The position of Indian immigrant professionals is further contextualised by Anannya Bhattacharjee who describes how, in the USA, Indians are regarded as 'a model minority, exemplifying high educational status and strong financial success' (Bhattacharjee, 1992:32). She suggests that this success results in the Indian immigrant bourgeoisie's 'selective amnesia' whereby the beginning of the history of the Indian community is commonly taken to date from the 1950s and 1960s when immigrants consisted predominantly of educated, urban professionals. This narrative, she argues, elides the earlier arrival of working-class Indian immigrants prior to World War I. It therefore, she suggests, 'limits [the Indian bourgeoisie's] response to other communities who continue to face more virulent forms of racism. And not infrequently intoxicated by its success as a model minority, it fails to perceive racism towards itself' (ibid.:33).

## The post-colonial migrant in metropolitan space

In a reading of Salman Rushdie's fiction, Gayatri Spivak argues that the post-colonial is divided between two identities, the migrant and the national; and that in Rushdie's fiction, the post-colonial migrant attempts to become the metropolitan and to redefine the nation (Spivak, 1989b:79). We see the same reconfiguration of identity in Mukherjee's neo-nationalist discourse, which is constituted not only by her fiction (and her comments on and readings of it) but also by the ways in which her writing has been used by critics and reviewers. However, as Spivak states in another context, transnationality is enabled and subtended by post-coloniality:

> those of us from formerly colonized countries are able to communicate with each other and with the metropolis, to exchange and to establish sociality and transnationality, because we have had access to the culture of imperialism. (Spivak, 1993:280)

Spivak observes that the diasporic elite disavows its own post-coloniality in the narratives it produces, as we see in Mukherjee's elision of her own class privilege in the new world of America. 'She wants to embrace the new', writes Craig Tapping, but 'the dilemma is that she also carries a lot of the old with her' (Tapping, 1992:43). Mukherjee identifies the UK and Canada with imperialism, and describes her decision to emigrate to the USA as a choice of freedom from imperialism: 'for me it was especially exciting to go to America because England to me connoted colonialism. It was associated with all that I had left behind' (Vignisson, 1992–93:156). In mythologising herself as a writer, she aims to construct herself as an American, and to reread her own experience as national or, more precisely, neo-national. In *The Middleman* it is Americans such as Marshall (in 'Loose Ends') and Jason (in 'Fathering')— Vietnam veterans displaced or challenged or both in their close contact with immigrants—who (like Bud in *Jasmine*) represent the old order, the old world within America, that is, the former 'nation'.

There is clearly a symbolic significance in Jasmine's remark that she sees 'a way of life coming to an end' with the demise of the Iowa farming community, and that what is being enacted is 'a final phase of a social order that had gone on untouched for thousands of years' (Mukherjee, 1990a:229); the influx of immigrants heralds the new social order.

Mukherjee's neo-nationalism—figured in the fantasy of the land of opportunity, and as the romance of the immigrant—is therefore the counter-narrative to her own diasporic condition and the dilemma of post-coloniality. She no longer wants to be 'post', because the India of *The Tiger's Daughter* and of her own childhood is, after all, 'past [its] prime' (Mukherjee, 1981:36). Wanting instead to be 'neo' and to identify with the centre, she in fact re-enacts its imperialist strategies in her appropriation of the label 'immigrant'. Mukherjee's neo-nationalism is what Spivak would call a 'species of collaboration with neocolonialism', whereby the post-colonial diasporic 'finds a nurturing and corroborative space [i.e. the literary canon] in this enclave in her attempts to remake history' (Spivak, 1989a:279).

The USA of Mukherjee's neo-nationalism is hyperreal in Jean Baudrillard's sense. 'When the real is no longer what it used to be', writes Baudrillard, 'nostalgia assumes its full meaning' (Baudrillard, 1983:8). Mukherjee's neo-nationalism is nostalgic because its function is to compensate for the absence of the real in the current demise and crisis of the USA as a global power. This would help account, of course, for the favourable reception of her work in the USA. Mukherjee's 'new pioneer' immigrants occupy the abandoned site of the 'real' in the national arena. The 'real' is reinvented in what Spivak calls 'the US semiotic field of citizenship and ethnicity' (Spivak, 1989a:279).

In her project to construct the 'real', Mukherjee becomes, in Baudrillardian terms, an 'ethnologist' of the immigrant. In her romance of the immigrant she exoticises character by taxonomising 'foreignness' in degrees of 'genuineness'. In this project, the immigrant as 'other' in the USA occupies the same site as the post-colonial diasporic in the country of origin. Tara, on her return visit to India in *The Tiger's Daughter*, feels like an alien: in her aunt's house she wonders, 'how does the foreignness of the spirit begin?'

(Mukherjee, 1987a:37). Jasmine and Du, on the other hand, are Bud's 'others'. Bud worries that they will 'never really have Du to [them]selves', because 'he'll always be attached in occult ways to an experience he can't fathom'; Jasmine thinks that her 'genuine foreignness frightens' Bud (Mukherjee, 1990a:231, 26). One of the characters in *The Middleman*—the banker Griff, who has an affair with a Filipina in 'Fighting for the Rebound'—is also confronted with the 'other'. 'There's a difference between exotic and *foreign*, isn't there?' he says. 'Exotic means you know how to use your foreignness, or you make yourself a little foreign in order to appear exotic. Real foreign is a little scary, believe me' (Mukherjee, 1990b:83).

These evocations of 'genuine foreignness', 'real foreign', and 'occult' experiences signal a preoccupation with reclaiming the real. As Brennan (1989) suggests, cosmopolitan authors write about the Third World but address a First World readership. They can be seen as 'informants' who commodify the Third World for First World consumption. In Mukherjee's case, those Third World migrants in metropolitan space constructed in her fiction are part of a hyperreal Third World, which constitutes what Spivak calls a 'comfortable "other" for transnational postmodernity' (Spivak, 1989a:275).

Ethnology is a mode of knowing in hyperreality. It is the means by which Mukherjee catalogues and names the 'real' (new) America, and reinvents a semiotics of American citizenship and ethnicity. Timothy Brennan praises Mukherjee for her cosmopolitanism and 'defiant challenge to traditional ways of conceiving the "national"' (Brennan, 1989:34). But he neglects to analyse the way in which she reconceives nationalism and reconstitutes the experiences of diverse constituencies into a new hegemony. Roger Rouse's analysis of Mexican immigrants' lifestyles in the USA offers an alternative model to Mukherjee's. Rouse resists the temptation to talk about migration in utopian terms as 'an inexorable move towards a new form of sociocultural order' such as neo-nationalism (Rouse, 1991:14). In this way he avoids the nostalgia of reconstituting a 'home'. In his study of Aguilillans living in the USA he claims that migration has produced 'neither homogenization nor synthesis. Instead, Aguilillans have become involved in the chronic mainte-nance of two quite distinct ways of life' (ibid.). This way of talking about the experience of immigration maintains the complexity of cross-cultural experience without romanticising the experience and thus subsuming and homogenising it. What Rouse in fact describes, as Khachig Tölölyan accurately observes, is the USA's 'inability to transform migrants into citizens' (Tölölyan, 1991:1). Rouse focuses on what Renato Rosaldo calls 'the implosion of the Third World into the first' (Rouse, 1991:17) and the manner in which migrants resist and transform the hegemonic social order. He does not mythologise 'what it is to become an American', as one of Mukherjee's reviewers does (Gorra, 1989:9). Nor does he homogenise postmodernity under the label 'America', as Mukherjee does when she writes: 'I believe that some people were meant to be American even if they never leave their village in Punjab—at heart, they are American' (Mukherjee, 1989:73).

It is significant that Rouse's study is based on precisely that constituency depicted in Mukherjee's fiction, namely what Brennan describes as 'the new immigrant underclass discovered eloquently in the writing of Mukherjee' (Brennan, 1989:34). Brennan himself contrasts the 'new immigrant underclass' with 'the other kind' of 'cosmopolitan'—the intellectual—which 'Mukherjee herself represents'. Yet he seems unaware of the slippage that occurs when the one speaks for the other. Mukherjee's representation of the diasporic, post-colonial and elite immigrant articulates a desire to be metropolitan, American, a 'new world citizen', and above all *not* to be a minority (Vignisson, 1992–93:160, 156). The 'immigrant underclass' is as much a fantasy for Mukherjee as Jasmine is: 'she's so gutsy, she has so much spirit, she's the kind of person I'd have wanted to be if I hadn't been as educated, as polite, as hesitant as I am' (ibid.:166).

The immigrant underclass exemplified by those Mexicans Rouse speaks about, however, enters the new world not with the privileges of the elite but as cheap and exploited labour. Consequently these people have an entirely different relationship to the metropolis and to transnational postmodernity. Mukherjee's mobility within the new world is of quite a different order. The contrast lends support to Spivak's conclusion that 'postcoloniality in general is not subsumable under the model of the revolutionary or resistant marginal in metropolitan space' (Spivak, 1993:64).

# Bibliography

Amos, V. and P. Parmar (1984) 'Challenging Imperial Feminism' *Feminist Review* 17, Autumn, pp. 3–19

Anderson, B. (1991) *Imagined Communities*, London: Verso

Ang, I. (1993) 'Migrations of Chineseness: Ethnicity in the Postmodern World' in Bennett (ed.) *Cultural Studies: Pluralism and Theory*, pp. 32–44

Appadurai, A. (1990) 'Disjuncture and Difference in the Global Cultural Economy' *Public Culture* 2, 2, Spring, pp. 1–24

Appiah, K. A. (1991) 'Is the Post- in Postmodernism the Post- in Postcolonial?' *Critical Inquiry* 17, Winter, pp. 336–57

Appignanesi, L. (ed.) (1987) *Identity: The Real Me: Postmodernism and the Question of Identity*, London: Institute of Contemporary Arts

Ariss, R. (1988) 'Writing Black: the construction of an Aboriginal discourse' in Beckett (ed.) *Past and Present: The Construction of Aboriginality*, pp. 131–45

Arthur, K. O. (1990) 'Beyond Orality: Canada and Australia' *Ariel* 21, 3, July, pp. 23–38

Ashcroft, B., G. Griffiths and H. Tiffin (1989) *The Empire Writes Back: Theory and Practice in Postcolonial Literatures*, London: Routledge

Attwood, B. and J. Arnold (eds) (1992) *Power, Knowledge and Aborigines*, Melbourne: La Trobe University Press in assoc.

with the National Centre for Australian Studies, Monash University

Barker, F., P. Hulme, M. Iversen and D. Loxley (eds) (1985) *Europe and Its Others*, vol. 1, Colchester: University of Essex

Barwick, D. (1974) 'And the Lubras are Ladies Now' in Gale (ed.) *Woman's Role in Aboriginal Society*, pp. 51–63

Baudrillard, J. (1983) 'The Precession of Simulacra' *Art and Text* 11, Spring, pp. 3–47

Beckett, J. R. (ed.) (1988) *Past and Present: The Construction of Aboriginality*, Canberra: Aboriginal Studies Press

Bell, D. (1991a) 'Interracial Rape Revisited' *Women's Studies International Forum* 14, 5, pp. 385–412

—— (1991b) Letter to the Editor *Women's Studies International Forum* 14, 5, pp. 505–13

Bell, D. and T. N. Nelson (1989) 'Speaking about rape is everyone's business' *Women's Studies International Forum* 12, 4, pp. 403–6

Benjamin, G. (1976) 'The Cultural Logic of Singapore's "Multiracialism"' in R. Hassan (ed.) *Singapore: Society in Transition*, Kuala Lumpur: Oxford University Press, pp. 115–33

Benjamin, W. (1973) 'The Storyteller' in *Illuminations*, New York: Schocken

Bennett, D. (ed.) (1993) *Cultural Studies: Pluralism and Theory*, Melbourne: Department of English, University of Melbourne

Benstock, S. (ed.) (1988) *The Private Self: Theory and Practice of Women's Autobiographical Writings*, London: Routledge

Berndt, C. (1985) 'Traditional Aboriginal oral literature' in Davis and Hodge (eds) *Aboriginal Writing Today*, pp. 91–103

Berndt, R. M. and R. Tonkinson (eds) (1988) *Social Anthropology and Australian Aboriginal Studies*, Canberra: Aboriginal Studies Press

Bhabha, H. K. (1983) 'The Other Question' *Screen* 24, 6, pp. 89–106

—— (1985) 'Signs Taken for Wonders: Questions of Ambivalence and Authority under a Tree Outside Delhi, May 1817' in Barker et al. (eds) *Europe and Its Others*, pp. 89–106

—— (1988) 'The Commitment to Theory' *New Formations* 5, pp. 5–23

—— (ed.) (1990) *Nation and Narration*, London: Routledge

—— (1994) *The Location of Culture*, London: Routledge

Bhattacharjee, A. (1992) 'The Habit of Ex-nomination: Nation, Woman and the Indian Immigrant Bourgeoisie' *Public Culture* 5, 1, pp. 19–44

Bird, D. and D. Haskell (eds) (1992) *Whose Place? A Study of Sally Morgan's* My Place, Pymble, NSW: Angus and Robertson

Birgin, V., J. Donald and C. Kaplan (eds) (1986) *Formations of Fantasy*, London: Methuen

Blaise, C. and B. Mukherjee (1977) *Days and Nights in Calcutta*, New York: Doubleday

—— (1987) *The Sorrow and the Terror: The Haunting Legacy of the Air India Tragedy*, Markham, Ontario: Penguin

Bottomley, G. (1992) *From Another Place: Migration and the politics of culture*, Cambridge: Cambridge University Press

Bottomley, G. and M. de Lepervanche (eds) (1984) *Ethnicity, Class and Gender in Australia*, Sydney: Allen and Unwin

Bottomley, G., M. de Lepervanche and J. Martin (eds) (1991) *Intersexions*, Sydney: Allen and Unwin

Brennan, T. (1989) *Salman Rushdie and the Third World*, New York: St Martin's Press

Brewster, A. (1989) *Towards a Semiotic of Postcolonial Discourse: University Writing in Singapore and Malaysia 1949–1965*, Singapore: Centre for Advanced Studies in assoc. with Heinemann

—— (1994) 'Oodgeroo: Orator, Poet, Storyteller' in A. Shoemaker (ed.) *Oodgeroo: A Tribute*, St Lucia, Qld: Australian Literary Studies, University of Queensland Press, pp. 92–104

—— (forthcoming) *Postcolonial and Ethnic Minority Literatures in English in Singapore and Malaysia*, Singapore: Singapore University Press

Brodzki, B. and C. Schenck (eds) (1988) *Life/Lines: Theorizing Women's Autobiography*, Ithaca and London: Cornell University Press

Burgmann, M. (1984) 'Black Sisterhood: The situation of Urban Aboriginal Women and their Relationship to the White Women's Movement' in Simms (ed.) *Australian Women and the Political System*, pp. 20–47

Burke, P. (1989) 'History as Social Memory' in T. Butler (ed.) *Memory: History, Culture and the Mind*, Oxford: Basil Blackwell, pp. 97–114

Butler, J. (1990a) 'Performative Acts and Gender Constitution: An Essay in Phenomenology and Feminist Theory' in Case (ed.) *Performing Feminisms*, pp. 270–82

—— (1990b) 'Gender Trouble, Feminist Theory, and Psychoanalytic Discourse' in Nicholson (ed.) *Feminism/Postmodernism*, pp. 324–40

—— (1993) *Bodies that Matter*, New York and London: Routledge

Carby, H. V. (1982) 'White woman listen! Black feminism and the boundaries of sisterhood' in Race and Politics Group, Centre for Cultural Studies (ed.) *The Empire Strikes Back: Race and Racism in 70s Britain*, Birmingham: University of Birmingham Centre for Contemporary Cultural Studies, pp. 212–35

Carter, P. (1987) *The Road to Botany Bay: an essay in political history*, London: Faber and Faber

—— (1992) *Living in a New Country: History, travelling and language*, London: Faber and Faber

Case, S. (ed.) (1990) *Performing Feminisms: Feminist Critical Theory and Theatre*, Baltimore: Johns Hopkins University Press

Castles, J. 1992. 'Tjungaringanyi: Aboriginal rock' in Hayward (ed.) *From Pop to Punk to Postmodernism*, pp. 25–39

Castles, S. and M. J. Miller (1993) *The Age of Migration*, London: Macmillan

Castro, B. (1992) 'Necessary idiocy and the idea of freedom' in Gunew and Longley (eds) *Striking Chords*, pp. 3–8

Chambers, I. (1990) *Border Dialogues*, London: Routledge

—— (1994) *migrancy, culture, identity*, London: Routledge

Chambers, R. (1984) *Story and Situation: Narrative Seduction and the Power of Fiction*, Minneapolis: Minnesota University Press

Chi, J. and Kuckles (1991) *Bran Nue Dae*, Broome and Paddington: Currency Press and Magabala Books

Chicago Cultural Studies Group (1992) 'Critical Multiculturalism' *Critical Inquiry* 18, pp. 530–55

Chua, C. L. (1992) 'Passages from India: Migrating to America in the Fiction of V. S. Naipaul and Bharati Mukherjee' in Nelson (ed.) *Reworlding the Literature of the Indian Diaspora*, pp. 51–61

Cixous, H. (1986) 'The Laugh of the Medusa' in Marks and de Courtivron (eds) *New French Feminisms*, pp. 245–64

Clare, M. (1978) *Karobran*, Chippendale, Vic.: Alternative Publishing Cooperative

Clifford, J. (1992) 'Travelling Cultures' in Grossberg, Nelson and Treichler (eds) *Cultural Studies*, pp. 96–112

Clifford, J. and G. E. Marcus (eds) (1986) *Writing Culture*, Berkeley: University of California Press

Cohen, P. and M. Somerville (1990) *Ingelba and the Five Black Matriarchs*, Sydney: Allen and Unwin

Collier, P. and H. Geyer-Ryan (eds) (1990) *Literary Theory Today*, Ithaca: Cornell University Press

Collins, J. (1984) 'Immigration and class: the Australian experience' in Bottomley and de Lepervanche (eds) *Ethnicity, Class and Gender in Australia*, pp. 1–27

Connor, S. (1989) *Postmodernist Culture: An Introduction to Theories of the Contemporary*, Oxford: Basil Blackwell

Cooper, C. (1993) *Noises in the Blood: Orality, Gender and the 'Vulgar' Body of Jamaican Popular Culture*, London: Macmillan

Couani, A. and S. Gunew (eds) (1988) *Telling Ways: Australian Women's Experimental Writing*, Adelaide: Australian Feminist Studies Publications

Cowlishaw, G. (1992) 'Studying Aborigines: Changing Canons in Anthropology and History' in Attwood and Arnold (eds) *Power, Knowledge and Aborigines*, pp. 20–31

Crawford, E. (1993) *Over My Tracks*, Ringwood, Vic.: Penguin

Daniel, H. (1988) 'The dark face of a woman's place', review in the *Age* of S. Morgan's *My Place*, reprinted in D. Hammond, M. O'Neill and J. Reid (eds) *Autobiography: The Writer's Story*, Fremantle: Fremantle Arts Centre Press, p. 17

Darian-Smith, K. and P. Hamilton (eds) (1994) *Memory and History in Twentieth-Century Australia*, Melbourne: Oxford University Press

Davies, C. B. (1992) 'Collaboration and the Ordering Imperative in Life Story Production' in Smith and Watson (eds) *De/Colonising the Subject*, pp. 3–19

Davis, J. and B. Hodge (eds) (1985) *Aboriginal Writing Today*, Canberra: Australian Institute of Aboriginal Studies

Daylight, P. and M. Johnstone (1986) *Women's Business: Report of the Women's Task Force*, Canberra: Australian Government Publishing Service

de Lauretis, T. (1984) *Alice Doesn't: Feminism, Semiotics, Cinema*, London: Macmillan

—— (ed.) (1986) *Feminist Studies/Critical Studies*, London: Macmillan

de Lepervanche, M. (1980) 'From Race to Ethnicity' *Australian and New Zealand Journal of Sociology* 16, 1, pp. 24–37

Deleuze, G. and F. Guattari (1983) 'What is a Minor Literature?' *Mississippi Review* 22, 3, pp. 13–33

Dirlik, A. (1994) 'The Postcolonial Aura: Third World Criticism in the Age of Global Capitalism' *Critical Inquiry* 20, pp. 328–56

Dodson, M. (1994) 'Towards the exercise of indigenous rights: policy, power and self-determination' *Race and Class* 35, 4, pp. 65–76

Donaldson, T. (1991) 'Australian Tales of Mystery and Miscegenation' *Meanjin* 50, pp. 341–52

During, S. (1987) 'Postmodernism or post-colonialism today' *Textual Practice* 1, pp. 32–47

—— (1992) 'Postcolonialism and Globalization' *Meanjin* 51, pp. 339–53

Edmund, M. (1992) *No Regrets*, St Lucia, Qld: University of Queensland Press

Fanon, F. (1968) *The Wretched of the Earth*, New York: Grove Press

Featherstone, M. (ed.) (1991) *Global Culture: Nationalism, globalization and modernity*, London: Sage

Felski, R. (1989) *Beyond Feminist Aesthetics: Feminist Literature and Social Change*, London: Hutchinson Radius

Felton, C. and L. Flanagan (1993) 'Institutionalised Feminism: A Tidda's Perspective' *Lilith: A Feminist History Journal* 8, Summer, pp. 53–9

Ferguson, R., M. Gever, Trinh T. Minh-ha and C. West (eds) (1990) *Out There: Marginalization and Contemporary Cultures*, Cambridge, Mass.: MIT Press and the New Museum of Contemporary Art

Ferrier, C. (1992) 'Aboriginal Women's Narratives' in C. Ferrier (ed.) *Gender, Politics and Fiction*, St Lucia, Qld: University of Queensland Press, pp. 200–18

Fesl, E. (1984) 'Eve Fesl' in Rowland (ed.) *Women who do and women who don't join the women's movement*, pp. 109–15

—— (1993a) 'Eve Fesl' in S. Rintoul (ed.) *The Wailing*, Port Melbourne, Vic.: Heinemann, pp. 339–41

—— (1993b) *Conned!*, St Lucia, Qld: University of Queensland Press

Fielder, J. (1991) 'Postcoloniality and Mudrooroo Narogin's Ideology of Aboriginality' *SPAN* 32, April, pp. 43–50

Fischer, M. M. J. (1986) 'Ethnicity and the Post-Modern Arts of Memory' in Clifford and Marcus (eds) *Writing Culture*, pp. 194–233

Fisher, B. (1977) 'Race and Class: Beyond Personal Politics' *Quest* 3, 4, Spring, pp. 2–14

Flick, B. (1990) 'Colonization and Decolonization: An Aboriginal Experience' in S. Watson (ed.) *Playing the State: Australian Feminist Interventions*, Sydney: Allen and Unwin, pp. 61–6

Foley, G. (1986) *Oral Tradition in Literature*, Columbia: University of Missouri Press

Foster, H. (ed.) (1987) *Postmodern Culture*, London and Sydney: Pluto Press

Foster, L. and D. Stockley (1984) *Multiculturalism: The Changing Australian Paradigm*, Clevedon, Avon: Multilingual Matters

Foucault, M. (1980) 'Two Lectures' in C. Gordon (ed.) *Power/ Knowledge: Selected Interviews and Other Writings 1972-1977*, New York: Pantheon, pp. 78–108

—— (1984) *The History of Sexuality*, vol. 1 [1976], Harmondsworth: Penguin

Fox-Genovese, E. (1982) 'Placing Women's History in History' *New Left Review* 133, May–June, pp. 5–29

Franco, J. (1989) 'The Nation as Imagined Community' in Veeser (ed.) *The New Historicism*, pp. 204–12

Frankenberg, R. (1993) *white women, race matters: the social construction of whiteness*, New York and London: Routledge

Friedman, S. S. (1988) 'Women's Autobiographical Selves: Theory and Practice' in Benstock (ed.) *The Private Self*, pp. 34–62

Gaffney, E. (1989) *Somebody Now*, Canberra: Aboriginal Studies Press

Gale, F. (ed.) (1974) *Woman's Role in Aboriginal Society*, Canberra: Australian Institute of Aboriginal Studies Press

Ganguly, K. (1992) 'Migrant Identities: Personal Memory and the Construction of Selfhood' *Cultural Studies* 6, pp. 27–49

Gare, N. (1987) 'Sally Morgan's *My Place*' *Westerly* 32, 3, pp. 81–4

Gates, H. L. (1991) 'Critical Fanonism' *Critical Inquiry* 17, pp. 457–70

Geiger, S. N. G. (1986) 'Women's Life Histories: Method and Content' *Signs* 11, pp. 334–51

Gilbert, K. (ed.) (1977) *Living Black*, Ringwood, Vic.: Penguin

Gilbert, P. (1988) *Coming Out From Under: Contemporary Australian Women Writers*, Sydney: Pandora

Gillet, S. (1991) 'At the Beginning: Ania Walwicz's Writing' *Southerly* 51, pp. 239–52

Gillis, J. R. (1992) 'Remembering Memory: A Challenge for Public Historians in a Post-National Era' *Public Historian* 14, 4, pp. 91–101

Gilroy, P. (1991) 'It Ain't Where You're From, It's Where You're At' *Third Text* 13, Winter, pp. 3–16

—— (1993) *The Black Atlantic: Modernity and Double Consciousness*, London: Verso

Goodall, H. (1987) 'Aboriginal history and the politics of information control' *Oral History of Australia Journal* 9, pp. 17–33

Goodwin, K. (1989) '"A Home that Is Right for Me": Bharati Mukherjee as an Indian Outsider' *Australian Journal of Politics and History* 35, pp. 407–13

Gorra, M. (1989) 'Call it Exile, Call it Immigration [review of B. Mukherjee, *Jasmine*]' *New York Times Book Review* 5 November, p. 9

Griffiths, G. (1989) 'Being there, being There: Postmodernism and Post-Colonialism: Kosinsky and Malouf' *Ariel* 20, 4, pp. 132–48

Grimshaw, P. (1980) 'Australian Women in History, Black and White: A Comparative Study' in *Second Women and Labour Conference Papers*, vol. 2, Victoria: Department of History, La Trobe University, pp. 692–704

Grossberg, L., C. Nelson and P. Treichler (eds) (1992) *Cultural Studies*, London: Routledge

Gunew, S. (1983) 'Migrant Women Writers: Who's on whose margins?' *Meanjin* 42, pp. 16–26

—— (1986) 'Ania Walwicz and Antigone Kefala: Varieties of Migrant Dreaming' *Arena* 76, pp. 65–80

—— (ed.) (1987) *Displacements 2: Multicultural Storytellers,* Geelong, Vic.: Deakin University Press

—— (1990a) 'Denaturalizing cultural nationalisms: multicultural readings of "Australia"' in Bhabha (ed.) *Nation and Narration,* pp. 99–120

—— (1990b) 'PostModern Tensions: Reading for (Multi)Cultural Difference' *Meanjin* 49, pp. 21–33

—— (1993) 'Multicultural Multiplicities: US, Canada, Australia' *Meanjin* 52, pp. 447–61

Gunew, S. and K. O. Longley (eds) (1992) *Striking Chords: Multicultural literary interpretations,* Sydney: Allen and Unwin

Gunew, S. and A. Yeatman (eds) (1993) *Feminism and the Politics of Difference,* Sydney: Allen and Unwin

Halbwachs, M. (1980) *The Collective Memory,* New York: Harper Colophon

Hall, S. (1987) 'Minimal Selves' in Appignanesi (ed.) *Identity: The Real Me,* pp. 44–6

—— (1989) 'The Meaning of New Times' in Hall and Jacques (eds) *New Times,* pp. 116–34

—— (1990) 'Cultural Identity and Diaspora' in Rutherford (ed.) *Identity,* pp. 222–37

Hall, S. and M. Jacques (eds) (1989) *New Times: The Changing Face of Politics in the 1990s,* London: Lawrence and Wishart

Hamilton, A. (1975) 'Aboriginal Women: The Means of Production' in Mercer (ed.) *The Other Half,* pp. 167–79

Hamilton, P. (1990) '"Inventing the Self": Oral History as Autobiography' *Hecate* 16, 1–2, pp. 128–33

—— (1994) 'The Knife Edge: Debates About Memory and History' in Darian-Smith and Hamilton (eds) *Memory and History in Twentieth-Century Australia,* pp. 9–32

Hancock, G. (1987) *Canadian Writers at Work: Interviews with Geoff Hancock,* Toronto: Oxford University Press

Hatzimanolis, E. (1993) 'Timing differences and investing in futures in multicultural (women's) writing' in Gunew and Yeatman (eds) *Feminism and the Politics of Difference,* pp. 128–42

Hayward, P. (ed.) (1992) *From Pop to Punk to Postmodernism,* Sydney: Allen and Unwin

Healey, B. (1988) 'Mosaic vs. Melting Pot' *New York Times Book Review* 19 June, p. 22

Hegeman, S. (1991) 'Shopping for Identities: "A Nation of Nations" and the Weak Ethnicity of Objects' *Public Culture* 3, 2, pp. 71–92

Heller, A. (1985) *The Power of Shame: a Rational Perspective*, London: Routledge and Kegan Paul

Hodge, B. and V. Mishra (1990) *Dark Side of the Dream: Australian Literature and the postcolonial mind*, Sydney: Allen and Unwin

Hollinsworth, D. (1992) 'Discourses on Aboriginality and the politics of identity in urban Australia' *Oceania* 63, pp. 137–55

hooks, b. (1990a) 'Talking Back' in Ferguson et al. (eds) *Out There*, pp. 337–43

—— (1990b) *Yearning: Race, Gender, and Cultural Politics*, Boston: South End Press

—— (1991) 'Writing Autobiography' in warhol and herndl (eds) *Feminisms*, pp. 1037–9

Hooton, J. (1990) *Stories of Herself When Young: Autobiographies of Childhood by Australian Women*, Melbourne: Oxford University Press

Horton, W. (1988) 'Australian Aboriginal Writers: Partially Annotated Bibliography of Australian Aboriginal Writers 1924–1987' in A. Rutherford (ed.) *Aboriginal Culture Today*, Sydney: Dangaroo

Hudson, W. and D. Carter (eds) (1993) *The Republicanism Debate*, Kensington: New South Wales University Press

Huggins, J. (1987) 'Black Women and Women's Liberation' *Hecate* 13, 1, pp. 77–82

—— (1991a) 'Writing My Mother's Life' *Hecate* 17, 1–2, pp. 88–94

—— (1991b) 'Towards A Biography of Rita Huggins' in Indyk and Webby (eds) *Memory*, pp. 143–64

—— (1993) 'Pretty deadly tidda business' in Gunew and Yeatman (eds) *Feminism and the Politics of Difference*, pp. 61–72

—— (1994) 'Respect vs Political Correctness' *Australian Author* 26, 3, pp. 12–13

Huggins, J. and K. Saunders (1993) 'Defying the Ethnographic Ventriloquists: Race, Gender and the Legacies of Colonialism' *Lilith: A Feminist History Journal* 8, Summer, pp. 60–9

Huggins, J. and I. Tarrago (1990) 'Questions of Collaboration' *Hecate* 16, 1–2, pp. 140–7

Huggins, J. and J. Willmot, I. Tarrago, K. Willetts, L. Bond, L. Holt, E. Bourke, M. Bin-Salik, P. Fowell, J. Schmider, V. Craigie and L. McBride-Levi (1991) Letter to the Editors *Women's Studies International Forum* 14, pp. 506–7

Huggins, R. and J. Huggins (1994) *Auntie Rita*, Canberra: Aboriginal Studies Press

Hutcheon, L. (1988) *A Poetics of Postmodernism: History, Theory, Fiction*, New York: Routledge

—— (1989) '"Circling the Downspout of Empire"; Post-Colonialism and Postmodernism' *Ariel* 20, 4, pp. 149–75

Huyssen, A. (1994) 'Monument and Memory in a Postmodern Age' in Young (ed.) *The Art of Memory*, pp. 9–17

Indyk, I. and E. Webby (eds) (1991) *Memory*, North Ryde, NSW: Angus and Robertson

Jacobs, J. M. (1989) '"Women Talking Up Big": Aboriginal women as cultural custodians, a South Australian example' in P. Brock (ed.) *Women, Rites and Sites: Aboriginal Women's Cultural Knowledge*, Sydney: Allen and Unwin, pp. 76–98

Jacobson, L. (1990) 'Reading Ania Walwicz' in Jurgensen (ed.) *Outrider* 90, pp. 148–59

Jakubowicz, A. (1984) 'Ethnicity, multiculturalism and neo-conservatism' in Bottomley and de Lepervanche (eds) *Ethnicity, Class and Gender in Australia*, pp. 28–48

JanMohamed, A. and D. Lloyd (1987) 'Introduction: Minority Discourse—What is to Be Done?' *Cultural Critique* 7, Fall, pp. 5–17

Jeyaretnam, P. (1987) *First Loves*, Singapore and Kuala Lumpur: Times Books

—— (1989) *Raffles Place Ragtime*, Singapore and Kuala Lumpur: Times Books

—— (1995) *Abraham's Promise*, Singapore: Times Books

Jurgensen, M. (ed.) (1990) *Outrider* 90, Brisbane: Phoenix

Kalantzis, M. and B. Cope (1993) 'Republicanism and Cultural Diversity' in Hudson and Carter (eds) *The Republicanism Debate*, pp. 118–43

Kaplan, C. (1992) 'Resisting Autobiography: Out-Law Genres and Transnational Feminist Subjects' in Smith and Watson (eds) *De/Colonising the Subject*, pp. 115–38

Katrak, K. H. (1989) 'Decolonizing Culture: Toward a Theory for Postcolonial Women's Texts' *modern fiction studies* 35, pp. 157–80

Keeffe, K. (1992) *From the Centre to the City: Aboriginal Education, Culture and Power*, Canberra: Aboriginal Studies Press

Kennedy, E. and T. Donaldson (1982) 'Coming Up Out of the Nhaalya: Reminiscences of the Life of Eliza Kennedy' *Aboriginal History* 6, 1–2, pp. 5–27

Kennedy, M. (1985) *Born a Half-Caste*, Canberra: Australian Institute of Aboriginal Studies

Kohn, H. (1971) *Nationalism: Its Meaning and History*, New York: Van Nostrand Reinhold

Kristeva, J. (1986) 'Woman Can Never Be Defined' in Marks and de Courtivron (eds) *New French Feminisms*, pp. 137–41

Kruger, B. and P. Mariani (eds) (1989) *Remaking History*, Seattle: Bay Press

Labumore (E. Roughsey) (1984) *An Aboriginal Mother Tells of the Old and the New*, Fitzroy, Vic.: McPhee Gribble/Penguin

Lacan, J. (1966) 'The Insistence of the Letter' *Yale French Studies* 36–7, pp. 112–47

Langford, R. (1988) *Don't Take Your Love to Town*, Ringwood, Vic.: Penguin

—— (Ginibi) (1991) 'Koori Dubays' in Spender (ed.) *Heroines*, pp. 129–41

—— (1992) *Real Deadly*, Pymble, NSW: Angus and Robertson

—— (1994a) 'Talking with Ruby Langford Ginibi [Interview with Janine Little]' *Hecate* 20, 1, pp. 101–21

—— (1994b) 'Nobby's Story' *Meanjin* 53, pp. 51–60

—— (1994c) *My Bundjalung People*, St Lucia, Qld: University of Queensland Press

—— (1994d) '"It is Our Turn": An Interview with Ruby Langford Ginibi [with Caitlin McGrath and Philippa Sawyer]' *Meridian* 13, 1, pp. 79–87

Langton, M. (1981) 'Urbanising Aborigines: The Social Scientists' Great Deception' *Social Alternatives* 2, 2, pp. 16–22

—— (1993) 'Well, I heard it on the radio and I saw it on the television. . .' North Sydney: Australian Film Commission

—— (1994) 'Aboriginal art and film: the politics of representation' *Race and Class* 35, 4, April–June, pp. 89–106

Larbalestier, J. (1990) 'The Politics of Representation: Australian Aboriginal Women and Feminism' *Anthropological Forum* 6, pp. 145–65

—— (1991) 'Through their own eyes: An interpretation of Aboriginal women's writing' in Bottomley, de Lepervanche and Martin (eds) *Intersexions*, pp. 75–91

Lattas, A. (1990) 'Aboriginal and Contemporary Australian Nationalism: Primordiality and the Cultural Politics of Otherness' in J. Marcus (ed.) *Writing Australian Culture: Text, Society and National Identity*, special issue of *Social Analysis* 27, pp. 50–69

—— (1992) 'Wiping the Blood off Aboriginality: The Politics of Aboriginal Embodiment in Contemporary Intellectual Debate' *Oceania* 63, pp. 160–4

Le Goff, J. (1992) *History and Memory* [1977], trans. S. Rendall and E. Claman, New York: Columbia University Press

Lee Kuan Yew (1964) 'Text of a Speech at the University of Singapore Society Dinner' *Tumasek* 3, September, pp. 18–19

Lewitt, M. (1992) 'Teething pains' in Gunew and Longley (eds) *Striking Chords*, pp. 67–9

Little, J. (1993) '"Tiddas in Struggle": A Consultative Project with Murri, Koori and Nyoongah Women' *SPAN* 37, December, pp. 24–32

—— (1994) Which Way: Directions in Recent Aboriginal Women's Prose, MA thesis, University of Queensland

Lorde, A. (1984a) 'The Master's Tools Will Never Dismantle the Master's House' *Sister Outsider*, New York: The Crossing Press, pp. 110–13

—— (1984b) 'The Uses of Anger: Women Responding to Racism' *Sister Outsider*, New York: The Crossing Press, pp. 124–33

Lucashenko, M. (1994) 'No Other Truth?: Aboriginal Women and Australian Feminism' *Social Alternatives* 12, 4, pp. 21–4

McCarron, R. (1991) Aboriginal Women's Writing: *Murditj yorka*—women of strength, MA thesis, Murdoch University

McClintock, A. (1992) 'The Angel of Progress: Pitfalls of the Term "Post-Colonialism"' *Social Text* 31–2, pp. 84–98

Marks, E. and I. de Courtivron (eds) (1986) *New French Feminisms: An Anthology*, Amherst: University of Massachusetts Press

Martin, B. and C. T. Mohanty (1986) 'Feminist Politics: What's Home Got to Do With It?' in de Lauretis (ed.) *Feminist Studies/Critical Studies*, pp. 191–212

Mascia-Lees, F. E., P. Sharpe and C. B. Cohen (1989) 'The Postmodernist Turn in Anthropology: Cautions from a Feminist Perspective' *Signs* 15, pp. 7–33

Mercer, J. (ed.) (1975) *The Other Half: Women in Australian Society*, Ringwood, Vic.: Penguin

Merlan, F. (1988) 'Gender in Aboriginal social life: A review' in Berndt and Tonkinson (eds) *Social Anthropology and Australian Aboriginal Studies*, pp. 15–76

Michaels, E. (1988) 'Para-ethnography' *Art and Text* 30, September–November, pp. 42–51

Mishra, V. (1994) 'The Diasporic Imaginary', a paper delivered in the Cultural Studies/Feminist Studies Colloquium at the University of California, Santa Cruz, 2 February

Mishra, V. and B. Hodge (1991) 'What is post(-)colonialism?' *Textual Practice* 5, pp. 399–414

Miyoshi, M. (1993) 'A Borderless World? From Colonialism to Transnationalism and the Decline of the Nation-State' *Critical Inquiry* 19, pp. 726–51

Mohanty, C. T. (1990) 'On Race and Voice: Challenges for Liberal Education in the 1990s' *Cultural Critique* 14, pp. 179–208

Morgan, S. (1987) *My Place*, Fremantle: Fremantle Arts Centre Press

—— (1988) 'A Fundamental Question of Identity, An Interview with Sally Morgan' [with Mary Wright] in A. Rutherford (ed.) *Aboriginal Culture Today*, Sydney: Dangaroo

—— (1989) *Wanamurraganya*, Fremantle: Fremantle Arts Centre Press

Morris, B. (1989) *Domesticating Resistance: The Dhan-Gadi Aborigines and the Australian State*, Oxford: Berg

Mudrooroo, (1992) 'A Literature of Aboriginality' *Ulitarra*, 1, pp. 28–33

—— (1994) 'Being published from the fringe' *Australian Author* 26, 3, pp. 15–17

Muecke, S. (1983) *Gularabulu: Stories from the West Kimberley by Paddy Roe*, Fremantle: Fremantle Arts Centre Press

—— (1988) 'Aboriginal Literature and the Repressive Hypothesis' *Southerly* 48, pp. 405–18

—— (1992) *Textual Spaces: Aboriginality and Cultural Studies*, Kensington: New South Wales University Press

Mukherjee, B. (1981) 'An Invisible Woman' *Saturday Night* 96, 3, pp. 36–40

—— (1986) *Darkness* [1985], Markham, Ontario: Penguin

—— (1987a) *The Tiger's Daughter* [1972], Markham, Ontario: Penguin

—— (1987b) *Wife* [1975], Markham, Ontario: Penguin

—— (1988) 'Immigrant Writing: Give Us Your Maximalists!' *New York Times Book Review* 28 August, pp. 1, 28

—— (1989) Interview *India Today* 15 February, p. 73

—— (1990a) *Jasmine* [1989], Markham, Ontario: Penguin

—— (1990b) *The Middleman and Other Stories* [1988], London: Virago

—— (1990c) 'passage from india' *Harper's Bazaar* Autumn, pp. 219–21

—— (1990d) 'An Interview with Bharati Mukherjee' *Iowa Review* pp. 7–32

—— (1993) *The Holder of the World*, London: Chatto and Windus

Murphy, J. (1986) 'The Voice of Memory: History, Autobiography and Oral Memory' *Historical Studies* 22, pp. 157–75

Nannup, A. (with L. Marsh and S. Kinnane) (1992) *When the Pelican Laughed*, Fremantle: Fremantle Arts Centre Press

Narogin, M. (1990) *Writing from the Fringe*, Melbourne: Hyland House

Nelson, C. and L. Grossberg (eds) (1988) *Marxism and the Interpretation of Culture*, London: Macmillan

Nelson, E. S. (ed.) (1992) *Reworlding the Literature of the Indian Diaspora*, New York: Greenwood

Nelson, T. N. (1991) Letter to the Editors *Women's Studies International Forum* 14, p. 507

Ngugi wa Thiong'o (1986) *Decolonising the Mind*, Nairobi: Heinemann Kenya

Nicholson, L. N. (ed.) (1990) *Feminism/Postmodernism*, New York: Routledge

Nora, P. (1989) 'Between Memory and History: *Lieux de Mémoire*' *Representations* 26, Spring, pp. 7–25

Olwig, K. F. (1993) *Global Culture, Island Identity: Continuity and change in the Afro-Caribbean community of Nevis*, Switzerland: Harwood

Ong, W. J. (1982) *Orality and Literacy: The Technologizing of the Word*, London and New York: Routledge

—— (1986) 'Text as Interpretation: Mark and After' in Foley (ed.) *Oral Tradition in Literature*, pp. 147–81

O'Shane, P. (1976) 'Is There Any Relevance in the Women's Movement for Aboriginal Women?' *Refractory Girl* September, pp. 31–4

Owens, C. (1985) 'The Discourse of Others: Feminists and Postmodernism' in Foster (ed.) *Postmodern Culture*, pp. 57–82

Papaellinas, G. (ed.) (1991) *Homeland*, Sydney: Allen and Unwin

Parry, B. (1987) 'Problems in Current Theories of Colonial Discourse' *Oxford Literary Review* 9, 1–2, pp. 27–58

Patel, V. (1989) 'Voyage of Discovery' *India Today* 15 February, pp. 72–3

Pearson, N. (1994) 'A troubling inheritance' *Race and Class* 35, 4, April–June, pp. 1–9

Perera, S. (1993) 'Response to Ien Ang' in Bennett (ed.) *Cultural Studies*, pp. 45–50

Perloff, M. (1986) *The Futurist Moment: Avant-Garde, Avant-Guerre and the Language of Rupture*, Chicago: University of Chicago Press

Personal Narratives Group (1989) *Interpreting Women's Lives: Feminist Theories and Personal Narratives*, Bloomington and Indianapolis: Indiana University Press

Pettman, J. (1992a) 'Gendered Knowledges: Aboriginal Women and the Politics of Feminism' in Attwood and Arnold (eds) *Power, Knowledge and Aborigines*, pp. 120–31

—— (1992b) *Living in the Margins*, Sydney: Allen and Unwin

Pilkington, D. (1991) *Caprice: A Stockman's Daughter*, St Lucia, Qld: University of Queensland Press

—— (1995) *Follow the Rabbit-Proof Fence*, St Lucia, Qld: University of Queensland Press

Raban, J. (1988) Review of *The Middleman, New York Times Book Review* 19 June, p. 1

Read, P. (1990) 'Come On In, The Water's Fine: Some Reflections of AHA Proposed Code of Ethics' *Australian Historical Association Bulletin* 64–5, pp. 33–42

Reagon, B. J. (1982) 'My Black Mothers and Sisters or On Beginning a Cultural Autobiography' *Feminist Studies* 8, 1, pp. 81–96

Richard, N. (1987–88) 'Postmodernism and Periphery' *Third Text* 2, pp. 5–12

Rivière, J. (1986) 'Womanliness as Masquerade' in Birgin, Donald and Kaplan (eds) *Formations of Fantasy*, pp. 35–44

Robbins, B. (1992) 'Comparative Cosmopolitanism' *Social Text* 31, 2, pp. 169–86

Rosaldo, R. (1989) *Culture and Truth: The Remaking of Social Analysis*, Boston: Beacon

Rose, D. B. (1992) 'Hidden Histories' *Island* 51, pp. 14–18

Rose, P. (1994) 'Poets Under the Influence' *24 Hours* January, pp. 74–9

Rouse, R. (1991) 'Mexican Migration and the Social Space of Postmodernism' *Diaspora* 1, 1, pp. 1–23

Rowland, R. (ed.) (1984) *Women who do and women who don't join the women's movement*, Melbourne: Routledge and Kegan Paul

Rowse, T. (1985) 'On the Notion of Aboriginality: A Discussion' *Mankind* 15, 1, pp. 41–55

—— (1993a) *After Mabo: Interpreting indigenous traditions*, Carlton: Melbourne University Press

—— (1993b) 'The Aboriginal Subject in Autobiography: Ruby Langford's *Don't Take Your Love to Town*' *Australian Literary Studies* 16, 1, pp. 14–29

Russ, J. (1983) *How to Suppress Women's Writing*, London: The Women's Press

Rutherford, J. (ed.) (1990) *Identity: Community, Culture, Difference*, London: Lawrence and Wishart

Safran, W. (1991) 'Diasporas in Modern Societies: Myths of Homeland and Return' *Diaspora* 1, 1, pp. 83–99

Safransky, R. (1992) 'The Goulash Archipelago' in Gunew and Longley (eds) *Striking Chords*, pp. 202–8

Sahlins, M. D. and P. V. Kirch (1992) *Anahulu: The Anthropology of History in the Kingdom of Hawaii*, Chicago: Chicago University Press

Said, E. (1985) 'Orientalism Reconsidered' in Barker et al. (eds), *Europe and Its Others*, pp. 14–27

—— (1987) 'Opponents, Audiences, Constituencies and Community', in Foster (ed.) *Postmodern Culture*, pp. 135–59

Sanders, M. A. (1994) 'Theorizing the Collaborative Self: The Dynamics of Contour and Content in the Dictated Autobiography' *New Literary History* 25, 2, pp. 445–58

Sandoval, C. (1991) 'US Third World Feminism: The Theory and Method of Oppositional Consciousness in the Postmodern World' *Genders* 10, Spring, pp. 1–24

Schiller, H. I. (1976) *Communication and Cultural Domination*, White Plains, New York: International Arts and Science Press

Scott, J. (1992) 'Multiculturalism and the Politics of Identity' *October* 61, Spring, pp. 12–19

Segal, D. A. and R. Handler (1992) 'How European is Nationalism?' *Social Analysis* 32, December, pp. 1–15

Seligman, C. (1986) 'From Calcutta to Iowa City' *Mother Jones* January, p. 38

Sharrad, P. (1990) 'Dear Emperor, There are a few things we need to discuss . . .' *Australian Book Review* 121, June, pp. 14–17

Shohat, E. (1992) 'Notes on the "Post-Colonial"' *Social Text* 31–2, pp. 99–113

Simms, M. (ed.) (1984) *Australian Women and the Political System*, Melbourne: Longman and Cheshire

Simon, E. (1978) *Through My Eyes*, Adelaide: Rigby

Skrzynecki, P. (ed.) (1985) *Joseph's Coat: An Anthology of Multicultural Writing*, Sydney: Hale and Iremonger

Slemon, S. and H. Tiffin (1989) 'Introduction' in *After Europe*, Sydney: Dangaroo, pp. ix–xxiii

Smith, A. D. (1986) *The Ethnic Origin of Nations*, London: Basil Blackwell

—— (1991) 'Towards a Global Culture?' in Featherstone (ed.) *Global Culture*, pp. 171–91

Smith, H. (1989) 'Outstanding Poetry: Writers in Recital: Sydney Art Perspecta 1989' *Age Monthly Review* 9, 6, September, pp. 6–8

Smith, Shirley (1977) 'Shirley Smith' in Gilbert (ed.) *Living Black*, pp. 246–51

Smith, Shirley with Bobbi Sykes (1981) *Mum Shirl*, Richmond, Vic.: Heinemann

Smith, Sidonie (1994) Getting a Life: The Everyday Uses of Autobiography in Postmodern America [unpublished work in progress, *Getting a Life*]

Smith, Sidonie and J. Watson (eds) (1992) *De/Colonising the Subject: The Politics of Gender in Women's Autobiography*, Minneapolis: University of Minnesota Press

Somerville, M. (1990) 'Life (Hi)story Writing: the relationship between talk and text' *Australian Feminist Studies* 12, Summer, pp. 29–42

Sommer, D. (1988) '"Not Just a Personal Story": Women's Testimonios and the Plural Self' in Brodzki and Schenck (eds) *Life/Lines*, pp. 107–130

Spender, D. (ed.) (1991) *Heroines*, Ringwood, Vic.: Penguin

Spivak, G. C. (1985) 'The Rani of Sirmur' in Barker et al. (eds) *Europe and Its Others*, pp. 128–51

—— (1987) *In Other Worlds: Essays in Cultural Politics*, New York and London: Methuen

—— (1988) 'Can the Subaltern Speak?' in Nelson and Grossberg (eds) *Marxism and the Interpretation of Culture*, pp. 271–313

—— (1989a) 'Who Claims Alterity?' in Kruger and Mariani (eds) *Remaking History*, pp. 269–92

—— (1989b) 'Reading *The Satanic Verses*' *Public Culture* 2, 1, pp. 79–99

—— (1990a) *The Post-colonial Critic: Interviews, Strategies, Dialogues*, ed. S. Harasym, New York and London: Routledge

—— (1990b) 'Poststructuralism, Marginality, Postcoloniality and Value' in Collier and Geyer-Ryan (eds) *Literary Theory Today*, pp. 219–44

—— (1991) 'Identity and Alterity—An Interview with Nikos Papastergiadis' *Arena* 97, summer, pp. 65–76

—— (1992) 'Teaching for the Times' *Journal of the Mid-West Modern Languages Association* 25, 1, pp. 3–22

—— (1993) *Outside in the Teaching Machine*, New York: Routledge

Steinberg, S. (1981) *The Ethnic Myth: Race, Ethnicity and Class in America*, New York: Atheneum

Strong, P. T. and B. Van Winkle (1993) 'Tribe and Nation: American Indians and American Nationalism' *Social Analysis* 33, September, pp. 9–26

Sussex, R. and J. Zubrzycki (eds) (1985) *Polish People and Culture in Australia*, Canberra: Department of Demography, Australian National University

Sykes, R. (1984) 'Bobbi Sykes' in Rowland (ed.) *Women who do and women who don't join the women's movement*, pp. 63–9

—— (1988) quoted in 'Five angry women with many wrongs to write' *Sydney Morning Herald* 3 September, p. 83

—— (1991) 'Black Women and the Continuing Struggle for Resources' in Spender (ed.) *Heroines*, pp. 179–86

Tapping, C. (1992) 'South Asia/North America: New Dwellings and the Past' in Nelson (ed.) *Reworlding the Literature of the Indian Diaspora*, pp. 35–49

Teh, C. W. (1979) 'City planning—emphasis is on quality' [speech given at the Seventh Annual Dinner of the Singapore Institute of Planners, Hyatt Hotel, 30 March]

Thorpe, M. (1991) '"Turned Inside Out": South Asian Writing in Canada' *Ariel* 22, 1, pp. 5–20

Thumboo, E. (1977) *Gods Can Die*, Singapore: Heinemann Asia

—— (1979) *Ulysses by the Merlion*, Singapore: Heinemann Asia

—— (1985) 'English Literature in a global context' in R. Quirk and H. G. Widdowson (eds) *English in the World: Teaching and Learning the Language and Literature*, Cambridge: Cambridge University Press, pp. 52–60

Tölölyan, K. (1991) 'In this Issue' *Diaspora* 1, 1, pp. 1–2

Torres, P. M. (1993) 'Patricia Gwen Torres' in R. Sykes (ed.) *Murawina: Australian Women of High Achievement*, Sydney: Doubleday, pp. 99–103

—— (1994) 'Interested in Writing about Indigenous Australians?' *Australian Author* 26, 3, pp. 24–5

Trees, K. (1992) 'Counter-Memories: History and Identity in Aboriginal Literature' in Bird and Haskell (eds) *Whose Place?*, pp. 55–65

—— (forthcoming) 'Postcolonial Pedagogy: The Politics of Postcolonial Reading Practices as They Relate to the Work of Aboriginal Writers' *Kunapipi*

Trinh, T. M. (1989) *Woman, Native, Other: Writing Postcoloniality and Feminism*, Bloomington and Indianapolis: Indiana University Press

—— (1990) 'Interview with Pratibha Parmar' *Feminist Review* 36, Autumn, pp. 65–74

Tucker, M. (1977) *If Everyone Cared*, Sydney: Ure Smith

van den Berg, R. (1994) *No Options. No Choice!*, Broome: Magabala

van Herk, A. (1991) *In Visible Ink: crypto-frictions*, Edmonton: NeWest Press

Veeser, H. A. (ed.) (1989) *The New Historicism*, London: Routledge

Vignisson, R. (1992–93) 'Bharati Mukherjee: An Interview' *SPAN* (special issue: Diasporas) 34–5, pp. 153–68

Walker, D. and T. Coutts (1989) *Me and You*, Canberra: Aboriginal Studies Press

Walker, K. (Oodgeroo Noonuccal) (1964) *We Are Going*, Brisbane: Jacaranda

—— (1977) 'Interview with Jim Davidson' *Meanjin* 36, pp. 428–41

Walwicz, A. (1981) 'Australia' in White and Couani (eds) *Island in the Sun*, pp. 90–1

—— (1982) *writing*, Melbourne: Rigmarole

—— (1985) 'europe' in Skrzynecki (ed.) *Joseph's Coat*, pp. 195–6

—— (1987) 'wogs' in Gunew (ed.) *Displacements 2*, p. 133

—— (1988) 'vampire' in Couani and Gunew (eds) *Telling Ways*, pp. 103–4

—— (1989a) *boat*, North Ryde, NSW: Angus and Robertson

—— (1989b) 'Statement' in D. Brooks and B. Walker (eds) *Poetry and Gender*, St Lucia, Qld: University of Queensland Press, pp. 69–70

—— (1991) 'Ania Walwicz' in Papaellinas (ed.) *Homeland*, pp. 191–5

—— (1992a) *red roses*, St Lucia, Qld: University of Queensland Press

—— (1992b) 'The Politics of Experience [Interview with Jenny Digby]' *Meanjin* 51, pp. 819–38

—— (n.d.[a]) 'Ania Walwicz' *Mattoid* 13, pp. 14–24

—— (n.d.[b]) 'The Writer, Writing: An Interview with Ania Walwicz' [with Ursel Fitzgerald] in *Introducing Ania Walwicz, Supplement to Mattoid* 28, pp. 2–23

Ward, G. (1988) *Wandering Girl*, Broome: Magabala

—— (1991) *Unna You Fullas*, Broome: Magabala

warhol, r. r. and d. p. herndl (eds) (1992) *Feminisms: an anthology of literary theory and criticism*, new brunswick, NJ: rutgers university press

Webb, H. (1991) 'Doin' the Post-Colonial Story? Neidjie, Narogin and the Aboriginal Narrative Intervention' *SPAN* 32, April, pp. 32–40

West, C. (1989) 'Black Culture and Postmodernism' in Kruger and Mariani (eds) *Remaking History*, pp. 87–96

West, I. (1987) *Pride Against Prejudice* Canberra: Australian Institute of Aboriginal Studies [1984]

Wheatley, N. (1994) 'Black and white writing: the issues' *Australian Author* 26, 3, pp. 20–3

White, D. and A. Couani (eds) (1981) *Island in the Sun: Anthology of Recent Australian Prose*, Glebe, NSW: Sea Cruise Books

Williams, R. (1983) 'The Culture of Nations' in *Towards 2000*, London: Chatto and Windus

Wright, P. (1985) *On Living in an Old Country*, London: Verso

Yap, A. (1971) *only lines*, Singapore: Federal Publications

—— (1977) *commonplace*, Singapore: Heinemann Asia

—— (1978) '"The Singapore Writer and the English Language"—A Comment' *RELC Journal* 9, 1, pp. 87–8

—— (1980) *down the line*, Singapore: Heinemann Asia

—— (1986) *Man Snake Apple and Other Poems*, Singapore: Heinemann Asia

Yeatman, A. (1993) 'Voice and representation in the politics of difference' in S. Gunew and A. Yeatman (eds) *Feminism and the Politics of Difference*, Sydney: Allen and Unwin, pp. 228–45

Young, J. E. (ed.) (1994) *The Art of Memory: Holocaust Memorials in History*, New York: The Jewish Museum

Young, R. (1990) 'Spivak: decolonization, deconstruction' in *White Mythologies: Writing History and the West*, London and New York: Routledge, pp. 157–75

# Index

*Compiled by Linda Browning*